American Catholic Heritage

Stories of Growth

William Barnaby Faherty, S.J.

Sheed & Ward

Sheed & Ward™ is a service of National Catholic Reporter Publishing Company, Inc.

Library of Congress Catalog Card Number: 90-64033

ISBN: 1-55612-417-1

Published by: Sheed & Ward
               115 E. Armour Blvd. P.O. Box 419492
               Kansas City, MO 64141-6492

To order, call: (800) 333-7373

Contents

Introduction

Through much of their history, American Catholics have had to face a two-front attack: from their fellow Catholics in other lands, especially churchmen, who said they could not be loyal Catholics and good Americans; and from their fellow Americans who said they could not be loyal Americans and good Catholics.

American Catholics loved their country. They rejoiced in the liberty it gave. The lands of their ancestors had not offered such assurance of freedom. Nor did the lands of those European Catholics who strongly criticized them. Catholics cherished equality under the law, the due process of the courts, the right to vote, and the freedom of speech, press and assembly they found in America.

They defended these privileges in all America's wars. One social commentator remarked: "Catholic America never produced an Arnold," in reference to the Revolutionary officer who went over to the enemy. American Catholics rejoiced because they had no King William of Orange or Czar Alexander III or Chancellor Otto von Bismarck to tell them how to worship God. Following the Constitution, American presidents knew religion lay beyond their political competence.

In another area, America's founding fathers solved a problem that baffled the great emperors and churchmen of Rome: the problem of succession of rulers. They cherished the memory of the Father of their country, President George Washington, who refused to accept the title of king when all other rulers were kings. He accepted the presidency for four years; and was willing to face the electorate when that time was over. After eight years he gladly turned the office over to a new president, even though a much less significant person, without the ordinary decline that often marked the late years of civil or ecclesiastical rulers-for-life.

American Catholics saw their country move through tragedies, such as the assassination of President Abraham Lincoln, without losing its great ideals of liberty enshrined in the Constitution. They saw safeguards in the dual separation of powers, the division within the central government between the lawmaking, the judicial and the executive functions, and the differentiation between the central government and the respective states on national or regional issues.

Catholics could participate in the selection of rulers and the making of laws. They knew the consensus of many was better than the dictates of one. The process of participation demanded their interest and concern. They had to study the issues before them.

American Catholics welcomed refugee priests from Catholic countries, such as France, South Germany, Austria, Italy, Mexico and Spain. They heard that so-called "liberal" regimes in those countries had confiscated schools, libraries and monasteries after expelling the members of the religious orders that conducted them. American Catholics may have faced hostility and misunderstanding from some of their neighbors in the States, but their government had respected their property and persons. The longest-enduring Jesuit seminary, for instance, was not in Europe or Latin America, but in the American midcontinent.

Even though the Church fared poorly in 19th-century Europe, European Catholics and especially Church authorities in Rome continued to question American traditions and laud the outmoded and confused European policies that regularly brought confiscation of Church property and sent religious men and women into exile.

In spite of hostility from neighbors at home and misunderstanding from Catholics in other lands, American Catholics on their part clung to their faith and their country. It is a story too rarely told in all its complexities.

1

The Colonies Oppose "Popery"

The depth of anti-Catholic hostility that marked much of early American history remains one of the major "unknowns" of the nation's past. Yet bitterness prevailed openly and almost universally in the colonial period and surfaced repeatedly after the foundation of the Republic. "Hatred of Catholics and foreigners had been steadily growing in the United States for more than two centuries," Ray Allen Billington, the expert on Protestant-Catholic tensions in the pre-Civil War period, wrote in his book *The Protestant Crusade 1800-1860*, published in 1938.[1]

The American colonists had come from an England that had just emerged from a century of religious turmoil. Henry VIII had taken his country out of the universal Christian Church; and then persecuted Catholics and Protestants alike who did not follow his whims. A period of confusion followed his death, with his Protestant son by his third wife ruling for a time, and then Catholic Mary Tudor, daughter of his first wife, the Spanish Princess Catherine of Aragon, succeeding him. Mary put to death many prominent Protestants, including Thomas Cranmer, the Archbishop of Canterbury.

Mary's half-sister and successor, Elizabeth, moved more cautiously and cleverly. She deplored the fanaticism of those Puritans who wanted to "purify" the Anglican Church of any surviv-

1

als of Catholic practice. But she also had personal problems remaining with the Church of her ancestors. To most of Europe, and to all Catholics everywhere, she was an illegitimate daughter of Henry VIII and, therefore, not rightfully Queen. She decided to revert to the Anglicanism of her half-brother, Edward's, reign.

A year after her accession to the throne, the Acts of Supremacy and Uniformity of 1559 excluded Catholics from the legal profession, from the universities and from teaching, banished priests under penalty of death and forced lay people to attend the Church of England or pay a heavy fine. Elizabeth sent many Catholics, such as scholar and author Edmund Campion, and the poet, Robert Southwell, to the hangman, but not on religious grounds. The courts condemned them to death as traitors, supporters of a "foreign potentate," the pope.

Many individual Catholics began to work to replace Elizabeth with Mary Stuart, Queen of Scots, the great-granddaughter of Henry VII, and legitimate heir of the Tudor dynasty. Some even connived with foreign powers to bring this about. When war broke out with powerful Spain, the champion of Catholicism at the time, the English government could readily cast suspicion on Catholics, even housewives like Margaret Clitherow, who was crushed to death for her Catholic faith.

The early reformers on the Continent had turned venomous language on the popes of the time, using chiefly the sometimes crude images of the Apocalypse. John Knox in Scotland and the Puritans in England matched the virulence of their continental counterparts. "Popery"—loyalty to the Popes—seemed to surpass all other crimes in England in the late 16th century.

When the colonization of America began early in the 17th century, the British Government introduced into colonial charters the same restrictions Catholics faced back home. The settlers on their part, Billington insisted, "reared in this atmosphere of intolerance, carried with them to the new land the same hatred of 'popery' that characterized the England of that day."[2]

The colony of Massachusetts, for instance, required an oath of allegiance that specifically denounced the Pope. A Catholic,

Sir George Calvert, Lord Baltimore, founded the colony of Maryland in 1634. He invited Catholics as well as Protestants to settle there and granted toleration to all. By 1654, only 20 years later, the Protestant majority repealed the Act of Toleration, and removed Catholics from equal protection of the law.[3]

The Massachusetts colonists denounced King James II's Act of Toleration, precisely because it included Catholics. They approved William's Act of Toleration a few years later that excluded Catholics from protection. But few Catholics ever reached the Bay Area in colonial times.

A number of Catholics found their way to New York during the governorship of Thomas Dongan, a Catholic appointed by King James II (1685-88). But the succeeding governor harried Catholics out of the colony. Even in Pennsylvania, the government forced the tolerant Quaker assembly to exclude Catholics from office.[4] Only in Rhode Island could a Catholic enjoy full civil and religious rights by 1700. "Even here," Billington wrote, "it is doubtful what the interpretation of the liberal statutes might have been."[5] In other New England colonies and the deep South, anti-Catholic legislation had no basis in reality. Almost no Catholics lived there. "Only the inherited bigotry of the Protestant settlers," Billington wrote, "motivated their enactment of penal statutes."[6]

The coming of William and Mary to the throne of England in 1688, and the beginning of the wars with France and Spain, added a new element. England and her colonies engaged in a succession of wars with these Catholic powers for almost a century. Any Catholic who turned up in the English-speaking colonies might seem a potential ally of armies of French Canada or Spanish Florida. "Americans," Billington concluded, "felt the same Catholic threat against their national existence that the English had felt in the days of Elizabeth."[7]

To put this English anti-Catholic legislation in focus, one must remember that all colonial governments looked to religious unity as part of their expansion programs. Canada and French Louisiana welcomed no Huguenots. As a matter of fact, these French Calvinists tried to start a colony of their own in Florida in the middle of the 16th century. Any Spaniard who turned Protestant left Spain for a Protestant country, not for the Spanish colonies. Swedes in Delaware were Lutherans. The Dutch in New York were Calvinists.

The restrictions on Catholics in English colonies took various forms. When Georgia sought settlers from Germany and Northern Ireland, it insisted that all be Protestants and appointed an inspector to see that no Catholics entered the colony. New York disarmed all its Catholic residents, thus automatically preventing them from seeking homes on the frontier. The French wars gave the New England colonies an added excuse for enforcing already-existing restrictions. Once-tolerant Connecticut removed Catholics from the protection of the laws in 1743, making it impossible for the Catholic Church to exist in that colony.

The Maryland legislature pursued a zig-zag course. At one time it prevented priests from teaching the young or performing the basic religious rites of baptism or the Eucharist. Later it allowed the priests to offer Mass and baptism in private homes. To curb Irish immigration as indentured servants, the one way most newcomers had to pay their Atlantic passage, the legislature put a heavy tax on Irish servants. So annoying were the "in-and-out" religious restrictions that the father of Charles Carroll of Carrollton, signer of the Declaration of Independence, seriously considered moving to French Louisiana shortly before the American Revolution.

"The hatred of Catholicism nurtured during the long period of French warfare," Billington noted, "was not allowed to die down after the Peace of Paris, for between 1763 and 1774, persistent propaganda was carried on, largely through the pulpit, which kept the people aroused against Popery."[8] Harvard began a lecture series to detect and expose the "idolatry, tyranny, damnable heresies, abominable superstitions and other crying wickednesses of the Roman Church." Little wonder a favorite fireside game in New England was called "Break the Pope's Neck."[9]

Quite interestingly this hostility to Catholicism played a part—albeit a minor one—in stirring up sentiment against the King at the start of the American Revolution. King George III granted freedom of religion to the Catholics in Canada and added the French settlements in the Ohio and Mississippi Valleys to the jurisdictions of the Province of Quebec. New Englanders saw a plot hatched by the King and the Pope to suppress their liberties. A prominent clergyman recalled many years later that he and his fellow New Englanders were ready to swear that the King had broken his Coronation Oath, betrayed his people and become a secret papist, an especially odious type.[10]

A brawl held annually in Boston on November 5, called "Pope's Day," ended with the burning of the Pope in effigy. Other colonies now took up this exercise as part of their fall "puberty rites." The President of Princeton University believed that the common hatred of Popery caused by the Quebec Act was the only thing that kept the divergent religious groups in the colonies sufficiently cohesive to fight the war for independence.[11]

In spite of this anti-Catholic atmosphere, the vast majority of colonial Catholics supported the Revolution. Unlike the British Isles where the Anglican Church had the privileged position and Catholics would still have to support it well into the succeeding century, the colonies were split religiously.

This was the religious situation in 1775, shortly after the Revolution began. Anglicanism was the established (the tax-supported) Church in the five southern states and the city of New York and the surrounding counties. But the Anglicans had no bishop resident in the colonies and aspiring ministers had to go to England for ordination. Any attempt on the part of the British government to appoint a bishop for America brought opposition from non-Anglicans as a further extension of the King's tightening control. Further, the estimated religious census in 1775 had placed membership second at half a million, 75,000 less than the Congregational body, the established Church in Massachusetts, Connecticut, and New Hampshire. Rhode Island and the Middle Atlantic States did not have an established church at that time.

The largest church groups that did not enjoy special status in any state were the Presbyterians on the frontier, estimated at 410,000 and the German Protestants in Pennsylvania, more

Calvinist than Lutheran, 200,000 in number. The Dutch Reformed congregations in New York and New Jersey claimed 75,000 adherents, the Quakers in Pennsylvania, New Jersey and Delaware 40,000, the Baptists and Catholics 25,000 each. Five thousand Methodists were scattered here and there and 2,000 Jews lived in New York and Rhode Island. The Methodists, a recent offshoot of Anglicanism, would soon make great headway, especially on the frontier. It is surprising that a mere 25,000 Catholics could have aroused such hostility.

2

The French Alliance
Reverses the Picture

This hostile attitude toward the Catholic Church shifted abruptly in 1778 when the French became allies, and mustered an army to sail for the American theater of war. A new mood began to grip the independent colonies. They began to accept the Catholics among them as sharers of the religion of their French friends. Now the British Empire Loyalists charged that the revolutionary colonists, by choosing Catholic France instead of Protestant England, had prepared the way for the establishment of Popery in America.

France's ally, Spain, which controlled the trans-Mississippi half of the continent, declared war on England in 1779, and Holland joined the alliance in 1780. Russia lined up all other countries in an attitude of passive hostility to Britain. England stood alone against the world. The Spanish Governor in New Orleans, Bernardo de Galvez, began a successful campaign that captured British posts at Baton Rouge and Mobile and launched a successful amphibious attack on Pensacola in the spring of 1781, thus checkmating British plans for the Mississippi Valley and the Gulf region. In the meantime, a large French Army under the Count de Rochambeau had landed in the colonies. In the fall of 1781, the combined French and American armies drove the British Commander Lord Cornwallis down the Virginia Peninsula toward the seaport of Yorktown. The French fleet cut off his escape route and forced his surrender.

7

England still had 54,000 troops in North America, 32,000 in the colonies. Fighting dragged on for more than a year. But England was losing worldwide, in India, in the West Indies and in the Mediterranean. The Tory regime of Lord North collapsed in March 1782, and a Whig ministry, more favorable to Americans, came in power. By 1783 Britain made peace.

Things were looking up for the colonies by that time and for the Catholics among them. Through the influence of such men as Charles Carroll of Carrollton, signer of the Declaration of Independence, Maryland had granted freedom of religion in 1777. Most of the other state constitutions still held restrictions on Catholics even when the states disestablished their churches.

The Federal Constitution, however, was to look in a different direction. Our Founding Fathers did not see need to give any special protection to one or other brand of Protestantism or to restrict Catholicism or other minority religions. It said: it is not the business of the state to determine the religion of any of its subjects. The First Amendment cut a new path in the struggle for religious freedom. In every other country in the world, at the time, and at almost all previous times, the sovereign exercised undue influence on the religious practice of his people.

The Constitution of the United States preferred no one church above others, as did most nations in the world, and encouraged all religious activities that conformed to the general social, ethical, and cultural outlook of the Republic.

In the 30 years after the signing of the Constitution, many states would follow the lead of the central government. Vermont dropped its restrictions on Catholics in 1786, South Carolina in 1790 and the New Hampshire legislature tried to do the same two years later. Delaware gave the vote to all free white males regardless of creed, and Georgia did away with its religious test for officeholders before the turn of the century. Connecticut disestablished Congregationalism in 1818, New York removed its oath objectionable to Catholics in 1822 and a decade later Massachusetts separated church and state.[1]

During these years Catholics in America were able to find a place for themselves in the wonderful country they had helped to create.

3

The Carrolls of Maryland

Much of the history of Catholicism in the early Republic centers around the illustrious name of Carroll. European-educated Charles Carroll of Carrollton came to the attention of his fellow Marylanders in 1773 when he criticized the governor's arbitrary taxation in a public debate in the *Maryland Gazette*. He was present at the First Continental Congress and a member of the Maryland Convention the following year. As a delegate to the Second Continental Congress in 1776, he stood in the brave band that signed the Declaration of Independence. He then went with Benjamin Franklin, Samuel Chase, and his cousin, Father John Carroll, on a special mission to French Canada.

He served in the Maryland Senate from 1777 to 1780, and took part in drawing up a new constitution that gave religious freedom. He served also in the United States Senate from March 4, 1789 to Nov. 30, 1792, and continued in the Maryland Senate for many years after that. He was to outlive all other signers of the Declaration of Independence.

A cousin, Charles "Barrister" Carroll, succeeded him as delegate to the Continental Congress in November 1776 and served in the Maryland Senate. Another cousin of the two Charles Carrolls, Daniel, took part in the national convention that drew up the United States Constitution in 1789, served in the Maryland Senate, and was elected to the First National Congress. President Washington assigned him to the committee that chose the permanent site of the new government in the District of Columbia.

Another cousin, Father John Carroll, who had gone with the delegation to Canada, had, like Charles Carroll of Carrollton, taken his education overseas. He remained in Europe and joined the Jesuits in 1753 at the age of 18. He worked in various assignments until the suppression of the Order in 1773. Returning to America, he did pastoral and missionary work during the years of the Revolutionary War.

In 1783 Father Carroll presented a plan of organization for the American clergy who gathered for a meeting at Whitemarsh, Maryland. Using his plan as a guide, the assembled priests, all ex-Jesuits, drew up a constitution to guide their ministries, and sent a petition to Pope Pius VI to confirm 64-year-old Father John Lewis, the former superior of the Jesuits, as head of the American mission. The petition and Carroll's covering letter showed that the clergy had definite ideas as to what the church in the New World should look like, and insisted on a native son as head of the American Church.

The authorities in Rome had toyed with many strange ideas, such as appointing a chaplain of Rochambeau's army as head of the Church in the newly independent colonies. Fortunately they avoided this mistake. At this juncture, American diplomat Benjamin Franklin, on a mission to Europe, used his influence in favor of his friend Father Carroll, who became "superior of the mission in the thirteen United States" in the summer of 1784.

Carroll disliked the manner of the appointment, as if a foreign power had taken too much influence in an internal affair of the United States. He found the restrictions on the faculties too limiting. He could employ, for instance, only priests approved and sent by a Roman congregation. This restriction disappeared as soon as Americans uttered a protest. Rome explained that the restrictions stemmed from the mistake of a scribe. This functionary had copied from a document intended for Central Africa.

Conscious that their countrymen were charting a course that reflected the aspiration of people for freedom and responsible government, Carroll and his priests wanted to create a church that would reflect the best of the American spirit. They recognized, too, that the externals of the church differed from country to country. "Bonnie Prince Charlie," as legitimate heir of the Stuart dynasty in Great Britain, had named the bishops of Ireland earlier in that century. The English government would soon have undue influence in the choice of Irish prelates. America wanted none of that.

Priests in some areas of the world selected their own bishops. Catholics in the east of Europe and the Near East had their own liturgical language and customs. Were Catholics in the new American federation less deserving of their own ways than these?

Communications were poor, especially during Europe's recurrent wars. Rome was far away, and had little knowledge of the vast new country across the ocean. Decisions had to be made promptly and from knowledge, not guesswork. It was ridiculous to expect a churchman in Rome who may never have left Italy to know what was best for Herkimer, New York. At that time, further, Rome had not yet set about centralizing the operations of the Church, nor had the popes become personally popular figures irrespective of their public policies. Those two tendencies would not become realities until the middle of the following century.

These American priests had as young men taken a pledge to go on any mission the pope would send them. In response to their oath of special loyalty, Pope Pius VI's predecessor Clement XIV had disbanded the Jesuit Order they belonged to, dispersed their members and imprisoned their Superior General without trial. They might not have seen Rome as a paragon of enlightened decision as many Catholics would tend to do a century later.

The American priests wanted the Church to respect their national identity and the spirit of America. They recognized the hatred of "popery" that had gripped other Americans. As a result they rightly believed that the less the hand of Rome hovered over religious affairs in America the better. They acknowledged that the Pope was spiritual head of the Church but held, as Carroll said, that "this was the only connection they ought to have with Rome."[1]

The priests wanted to avoid any foreign jurisdiction, even that of a Roman congregation, such as the Office of the Propaganda that controlled mission affairs. They asked religious liberty, the election of a bishop from among their own priests, and the recognition of America as equal with other countries. Caught up in the enthusiasm of the birth of a nation, they wanted to create a distinct pattern of church life, different from that of Europe's state-controlled or regulated churches. They advocated freedom of religion and accepted separation of Church and State. They hoped to give the world a splendid example of living harmoniously with members of other Christian denominations. Carroll considered the use of English in the liturgy and welcomed wide lay activity. He expressed these views in personal letters to priest friends rather than in official correspondence with Rome.[2]

A majority of the priests were convinced that America needed a bishop. They had one worry, however. Would the country welcome such a functionary, so reflective of the old ways of Europe? The pleasant reception of William White in 1787 as Protestant Episcopal Bishop of Pennsylvania eased this worry. A petition went to Rome in March 1788.

Rome answered four months later, leaving to the priests of America the choice of the See of the bishop, the decision whether he would be titular or ordinary, and the selection of the man. The Apostolic See would confirm their choice. Carroll was consecrated in England in August 1790.

4

The First Bishops

One might have expected John Carroll, as an ex-Jesuit, to place high priority on education. He looked immediately to the education of candidates for the priesthood. He wanted them trained in the United States, not in European seminaries. He negotiated with French priests of the Order of St. Sulpice in the fall of 1790. They began St. Mary's Seminary in Baltimore the following summer.

He worked hard also to open Georgetown Academy for pre-seminary and lay students, successfully soliciting funds from the wealthy Catholic gentry. The school welcomed its first student in 1791. A few years later a small group of dedicated Catholic women began the Georgetown Visitation Academy, the first Catholic women's school in American territory.

Other plans of Carroll faced too many obstacles. The country did not have enough native priests. While priests were willing to come from Europe, many of them were to prove out of harmony with the American spirit as Carroll reflected it. Others had gotten into trouble at home, and would cause trouble in America. Some never learned the language. Some excellent men intended to return to Europe after a few years on the American mission. Others were wanderers who could not stick to a task.

Communication with Rome, slow at best, became impossible with Europe's endless wars. Carroll, for instance, wanted Father Lorenz Graessl as his Coadjutor Bishop. By the time word arrived that Rome had confirmed this appointment,

Graessl had died ministering to the sick in an epidemic in Philadelphia. With the Pope imprisoned by Napoleon, Carroll did not receive word of ratification of his second choice, Leonard Neale, for six years. Bishop Neale lacked the gifts to carry out Carroll's vision—even if he had seen it. Unfortunately he did not and few others did either.

As early as 1792 Carroll thought of dividing the diocese. But not until 1808 did the actual division take place. Fortunately two outstanding French priests, Fathers de Cheverus and Flaget, were available. Jean Lefevere de Cheverus, who had escaped from the dungeons of the French Revolution and come to America, had worked for eight years among Penobscot Indians and whites in Maine and Massachusetts. As bishop he moved as easily in Boston society as Carroll did in Baltimore. He guided the church in Massachusetts and surrounding states for 15 years before returning to his native land where he became a cardinal of the church and a peer of France.

Benedict Joseph Flaget, S.S., who had spent time as a missionary in Indiana, as professor at Georgetown and at St. Mary's Seminary in Baltimore, established the faith solidly among the Maryland pioneers in central Kentucky as Bishop of Bardstown during the ensuing 42 years.

Carroll recommended an Irish Franciscan, Michael Egan, for Philadelphia, but the man lacked strength of body and purpose. Conflicts in the diocese brought him to an early grave four years later. Carroll hesitated to name a man for New York, and Rome stepped in to name a Dominican, Richard Luke Concanen, recommended by the hierarchy of Ireland. Concanen died before he reached the States and Rome appointed another Dominican chosen by the Irish hierarchy, John Connolly, a total stranger to Carroll and the United States. Italian prelates ordained him before he left Italy. Carroll rightly feared the consequence of this "dangerous precedent." The next appointment was even worse. Rome delayed six years in approving a bishop for Philadelphia and then appointed Henry Conwell, vicar-general of the archdiocese of Armagh in Ireland, a man almost 75 years of age. Irish politics suggested exile, and he chose Philadelphia over Madras in southeast India. Troubles lay ahead for the city of Brotherly Love.

By that time, the Napoleonic wars were over; Pius VII had returned to Rome; the curia was functioning again in its traditional slow gear; centralization was underway.

5

The French Residents of the Mississippi Valley

While 11 ex-Jesuits were working in a limited area along the Atlantic seaboard during the American Revolution, the 12th priest in what became American Territory, the French Canadian Pierre Gibault, Pastor at Kaskaskia in the Illinois Country, had to cover an area bigger than France. Bishop Jean Olivier Briand of Quebec had given him quasi-episcopal powers for the entire Northwest Territory. Yet he had quietly refused to go along with the bishop in supporting the English cause, even though the Quebec prelate had threatened him with the excommunication of all French Canadians who supported the English-speaking colonies in their Revolution.

When George Rogers Clark reached Kaskaskia with his Kentucky riflemen in 1778, Pierre Gibault supported him, helped to supply the Kentuckians, and convinced his own parishioners in Kaskaskia and those in Vincennes on the Wabash that the future lay with the Americans.

This action put him in double jeopardy: with his bishop who opposed his action; and with the British commander at Detroit, Henry Hamilton, who listed Gibault as a traitor. The victory of the Americans and their allies removed Gibault from the shadow of Hamilton's hangmen. But his church position was not totally clear. Bishop Briand ignored him. Carroll sent two different French-speaking priests to the area, one with the power of vicar-general. Gibault wondered who was in charge. He eventually found out.

In October 1788 Rome transferred the Illinois country from Canadian to American jurisdiction. And a year after Carroll's consecration as bishop, Rome made his diocese coterminus with the boundaries of the United States. Unfortunately, neither the United States nor the American church ever gave proper credit to Pierre Gibault for his tremendous work during a third of a century.

Except for a few settlers in the Old Northwest Territory, at Detroit, at Vincennes on the Wabash, at Prairie du Chien along the Upper Mississippi, at Cahokia across the river from St. Louis, and at Kaskaskia 50 miles farther south, the majority of French in the Mississippi Valley did not become part of the United States until the Louisiana Purchase of 1803. This doubling of American territory brought into the Union a large concentration of French-speaking Lower Louisiana Catholics in the area of New Orleans and in the Bayou country 100 miles to the west.

The main city of the Louisiana Territory, New Orleans boasted of a cathedral built early in the previous decade, and a century-old Ursuline Convent and school. A bishop, Luis Penalver y Cardenas, who had arrived as religious leader of Louisiana Territory in 1795, had served there until 1801 when he left to become Archbishop of Guatemala.

A few residents of Lower Louisiana had recently come from France, refugees of the Revolution, but more of them had come long before from French Canada, as had Bienville, the founder of the city. In the Bayou country 100 miles west, a large body of "Acadians," informally dubbed "Cajuns," had settled. The British troops had forcibly expelled them from their homes in Acadia (later to be called Nova Scotia) at the start of the French and Indian War 45 years before.

The French Catholic residents of Lower Louisiana stretched through all classes of society: rice planters, manufacturers, business and professional people, ship owners, small farmers, muskrat trappers, fishermen, "free men and women of color" and slaves. The French slave code, less severe than the English or Spanish, obliged owners to educate their servants in the tenets of Christianity. That so many French-speaking blacks were Catholic seemed to confirm the presumption that the French masters kept that prescription of the code.

When this territory became the state of Louisiana in 1812, it provided a Catholic center at the southwestern part of an otherwise Anglo-Saxon Protestant South to match the Maryland Catholic community at the northeast corner of southern states.

A much smaller but regionally influential group of French Catholics came into the Union in upper Louisiana, eventually to be the state of Missouri. As with their fellow countrymen farther south, the Catholic Church had been the established church among them for 40 years. They never knew the hostility that Catholics faced in the English colonies along the Atlantic coast. In the area of St. Louis, several well-educated and highly successful businessmen of French background, such as Auguste and Pierre Chouteau, Regis Loisel, and Francois Benoist, took part in making St. Louis the commercial depot of the Central Valley, the hub of steamboat transportation later on, and the Gateway of the West. In 1818 the brilliant and imaginative Bishop of Louisiana Territory, Louis W.V. DuBourg, descendant of West Indian planters, and a refugee of the French Revolution, temporarily made his residence in St. Louis and brought a number of educators and missionaries, men and women from Belgium, France and Italy, to the area.[1]

The most noted of these missionary-educators who came to America under the inspiration of Bishop DuBourg, Saint Philippine Duchesne of the Religious of the Sacred Heart, now a canonized saint of the Church, began the first school for girls west of the Mississippi. She also taught native American girls and spent a year among the Potawatomi in Kansas Territory. But her greatest contribution was the solid establishment of her religious institute in Missouri and Louisiana.

Bishop DuBourg began St. Louis Academy, the forerunner of St. Louis University, under the direction of Father Francois Niel, a young French priest, and a seminary under the guidance of Father Felix de Andreis, C.M. Another of DuBourg's Vincentian recruits, Father Joseph Rosati, began the first college chartered in the trans-Mississippi region, and became first bishop of St. Louis.

Twenty years later, Sisters of St. Joseph came from France to the French village of Carondelet near St. Louis and opened several schools for girls. With a grant from the state of Missouri, specially-trained nuns under the direction of Mother Celestine Pommerel began the first school for the deaf in the West, an institution destined to continue through the succeeding decades. The Sisters of St. Joseph would grow rapidly, as the years passed, to become one of the largest religious institutes in the nation, with schools in widespread areas.

Pierre Menard, a Canadian merchant-capitalist who lived on the Illinois side of the river at Kaskaskia, took part in business enterprises with his fellow French in St. Louis. An Illinois territorial delegate, he was elected first lieutenant-governor when Illinois became a state in 1818, one of the highest positions held by a Catholic at the time outside of Maryland or Louisiana. Colonel Menard invited the Visitation Sisters of Georgetown, under the leadership of Mother Agnes Brent, to open a school for girls in Kaskaskia in the early 1830s. Four years later he helped them build a four-story brick structure called Menard Academy, the finest girls' school in Illinois at the time.[2]

French mountain men went out from the area of St. Louis to open the West: among them Pierre Vial, founder of the Santa Fe Trail, and Henry Chatillon, guide of author Francis Parkman to Oregon.

Most of the original residents of St. Louis had come from Canadian settlements rather than directly from France. In the 19th century, few French nationals would reach St. Louis. But several prominent colonial families came from the French West Indies. Among them were parents of Union officers in the Civil War, Colonel Julius Garesche and Brigadier General Rene Paul.

The early French in Missouri welcomed Anglo-Americans. They gave to their fellow Catholics from Ireland a place of freedom and opportunity unavailable elsewhere in the English-speaking world, including Dublin itself, still burdened by England's penal laws.

Numerous St. Louis Irish had already gained an established place in business and government before the large numbers of immigrants driven from Ireland by the famine met hostility and rejection in Atlantic coastal cities.

Many children of the early French intermarried with these newcomers. The wife of Alexander McNair, the first Missouri governor, was of a French colonial family. A popular and enterprising young businessman, Edward Walsh, married Isabelle, daughter of Viscount Jules de Mun, a refugee of the Revolution. Later generations of St. Louisans could boast of ancestry from both St. Louis pioneer Auguste Chouteau and General William Clark, from John Mullanphy, St. Louis' first Irish-born man of wealth, and Firmin Desloge, a Missouri mineral magnate.

As a result of the attitudes and characteristics of the founding French settlers, Catholicism was to grow in St. Louis, the second archdiocese in the United States, and the main city of the middle west by mid-century, with a confidence unknown in other parts of the country during the 19th century. Of the priests, diocesan or religious, who worked in the city early in their careers, seventeen became bishops and four archbishops in 20 different sees during that time.

All the while, far to the Southwest, in Texas, New Mexico, Arizona and along the California coast, Franciscan missionaries had nurtured the faith among native Americans and Spanish colonists for centuries. These territories would become part of the United States a few decades later.

6

Catholics in the Era of Good Feeling

The two terms of President James Monroe (1816-1824) won the nickname the Era of Good Feeling. Those years immediately after the War of 1812 were certainly that for the French-speaking Catholics of the Mississippi Valley, the Catholics of Maryland, some of whom were moving to Kentucky and the West, and the scattering of their coreligionists in the middle Atlantic states, especially in Pennsylvania and New York.

A new dimension, sanctity, had come into the American Catholic community in the early decades of the century. The daughter and granddaughter of extremely dedicated Christian people, Elizabeth Bayley Seton had, as a young wife and mother, engaged in charitable work for widows and orphans in the late years of the 18th century. Shortly after her husband died in 1805, she became a Catholic. She moved from New York to Baltimore to teach school and support her five children.

Eventually she adopted the rule of St. Vincent and began a new institute, the Sisters of Charity. She opened the first free parochial school in the United States in Emmitsburg, Maryland In 1814 she sent sisters to open an orphanage in Philadelphia and another in New York. From these two ventures sprang an amazing network of hospitals, child-care centers, clinics, homes for the aged, social welfare centers and mental health installations.

Across the Appalachians in the state of Kentucky three new religious congregations had taken root during the War of 1812: the Dominicans, the Charities of Nazareth and the Sisters of Loretto at the Foot of the Cross. The zealous Belgian-born missionary, Father Charles Nerinckx, directed the last of these groups, with Sister Mary Rhodes the pioneer superior.

Shortly after the war, Vincentians from Italy, recruits of Bishop DuBourg, began a seminary and college among Maryland and Kentucky-born Catholics at Perryville, MO. Father Joseph Rosati, C.M., directed this combined institution until he became Bishop of St. Louis in 1826.

While the War of 1812 was still on, the President of Harvard, in the Dudleian lecture for 1813, saw hope for Catholics. This was a tremendous change from the content of earlier messages. Ten years later the General Court of the Commonwealth of Massachusetts invited a Catholic priest, William Taylor, to open the session with an invocation. Virgil Barber, a promising young Episcopalian pastor, came into the Church with his entire family. He and his son became Jesuit priests and his wife and daughters nuns.[1] A cousin, William Tyler, became a convert in 1823 at the age of 18, and Bishop of Hartford 20 years later.[2]

In view of later court decisions that looked to a "wall of separation between church and state"—a term not found in the Constitution, but in a personal letter of Thomas Jefferson—it is hard to appreciate the harmonious cooperation between the national government and religious bodies in the days of the early Republic.

A program instituted by Secretary of War John C. Calhoun in the days of President James Monroe, for instance, typified this working together of state and church. The government offered a subsidy to all religious, educational and philanthropic organizations that had practical plans for the improvement of the lot of the native Americans. Baptists in several places, Quakers in Pennsylvania, the United Brethren of North Carolina, the Methodists of South Carolina, and the Catholic Bishop of Louisiana Territory applied for and received grants.

Bishop Louis W.V. DuBourg, who in the 1790s had been head of Georgetown University, proposed to President James Monroe the establishment of a combined Indian school and clerical seminary near the confluence of the Missouri and Mississippi Rivers. He offered a fertile plantation near the French village of Florissant, Missouri, and invited a group of young Belgian Jesuit seminarians, then located in Maryland, to move there. With the encouragement of General William Clark, Indian Commissioner, Secretary of War John C. Calhoun, then in charge of government relations with native Americans, granted the subsidy. The young Belgians took a wagon to Wheeling, a flatboat down the Ohio, and hiked across southern Illinois to St. Louis. Shortly after they settled in Florissant, Sauk, Ioway and Osage boys attended the school and continued to come during the next few years. Thus began the first Catholic missionary effort among native Americans in the new republic. The year proved to be the 150th anniversary of Father Marquette's visit to the area in 1673.

Three great religious thrusts stemmed from this Jesuit seminary: an impressive missionary effort among Indians of the plains and the Rockies; a parochial apostolate, especially among German Catholics in towns in the Lower Missouri River Valley; and the chartering of St. Louis University in 1832, an institution that spawned five midwestern Catholic universities in the succeeding half-century.

But that was not the only instance wherein the federal government supported Bishop DuBourg's educational efforts. He had begun the first community school in St. Louis. At the urging again of Commissioner William Clark, the government paid the tuition for the son of Sacajawea, the Shoshone girl who had been so valuable to the Lewis and Clark expedition. The town government, too, financed the education of other poor boys at the school.

The decades of the 1820s and 1830s saw the development of new dioceses: Richmond, Virginia and Charleston, South Carolina in 1820, Cincinnati in 1821, New Orleans and St. Louis in 1826, Mobile in 1829, Detroit in 1833, Vincennes, Indiana in 1834, Dubuque, Iowa and Nashville, Tennessee in 1837.

A few of the early bishops were born in Maryland: Edward Fenwick, O.P., of Cincinnati, Benedict J. Fenwick, S.J., of Boston, and Samuel Eccleston of Baltimore. Would that the country had produced more native sons available for leadership!

The Irish bishops had recommended several priests for bishoprics in America who found the American scene beyond their comprehension and competence. The Irish ecclesiastics more than compensated for these misjudgments by recommending in 1820 the Secretary of the Diocese of Cork, educator and editor, Father John England, for the diocese of Charleston in South Carolina. Like Washington and Jefferson many years before, John England had fought for freedom during the 60 year reign of George III, whose mind may have gone but whose tyranny lingered on. Of all bishops, John England's views most reflected those of John Carroll. He set out resolutely as Carroll had done to build a truly American Church.

When he became bishop of the Carolinas and Georgia in 1820, John England developed a constitution for his diocese. It provided for the annual election of a board of trustees by the men of the parish. This board met regularly throughout the year, with the local pastor acting as president. In some areas of decision he had no veto power. In general, the board concerned itself with the business matters of the parish. Bishop England felt that this program combined the best of American and universal Catholic traditions. It was similar to what Catholics saw working in the parishes of their Protestant neighbors.

"England also defined the Church," historian Jay P. Dolan wrote, "in a more republican, less monarchical, manner than most of his contemporaries."[3] He advocated separation of church and state, religious liberty and freedom of conscience, a republican form of church government with local church councils and the trustee system. He emphasized the church as a congregation of the faithful rather than as an institution. Unfortunately John England was 140 years ahead of his times, and equally apart from so many of his fellow bishops who had come to America but had failed to imbibe its spirit.

England seemed to have success in an area where so many others failed: the area of lay activity. Instead of cooperation between pastors and people, the all-too-often pattern in those years was rivalry, hostility, even in some instances outright violence. Blame for these difficulties could rightly be attributed to both sides, not equally in every instance.

A number of bishops came from France, many of them refugees of the French Revolution and members of the Society of St. Sulpice, designated by the initials S.S., and dedicated to the training of priests. Among these men of France were the already-mentioned John Cheverus of Boston; Benedict J. Flaget, S.S., of Kentucky; Louis W.V. DuBourg, S.S., of Louisiana Territory; DuBourg's recruits for service in America, Michael Portier of Mobile, and Anthony Blanc of New Orleans; John Dubois, S.S., of New York; Guy I. Chabrat, S.S., coadjutor in Bardstown, and his successor, John Baptist David, S.S.; Ambrose Marechal, S.S., of Baltimore; Simon Brute, S.S., of Vincennes; and his successor, Celestine R. De La Hailandiere; Mathias Loras of Dubuque; and J.J.M. Chance, S.S., of Natchez.

Bishop DuBourg also recruited for the Louisiana Territory two Vincentian educators and missionaries: Leo DeNeckere, C.M., who became Bishop of New Orleans, and Joseph Rosati, C.M., first Bishop of St. Louis. According to an historian of the American Church, Peter K. Guilday, Rosati's fellow bishops recognized him as "one of the most remarkable bishops in Christendom."[4] A writer for the *Italian Americana* praised Rosati as Italy's greatest contribution to the United States.[5] In the territory he so zealously shepherded, the Church eventually created, in whole or in part, a total of 44 dioceses.

7

Heavy Catholic Immigration Brings Changes

Roughly 85% of Americans at the time of the American Revolution claimed British (English, Scotch, or Scotch-Irish) background and considered themselves Protestants, even those not explicitly church members. The few Catholics in Maryland and the middle Atlantic colonies hardly affected this pattern. The Catholic Church in America was moving along quietly and steadily in this atmosphere following the War of 1812. But this peace was not to endure.

Change came by the early 1840s as a result of immigration from Ireland and Germany that doubled and tripled during the ensuing decades. Irish immigrants, most of them Catholic, numbered 39,403 in 1840. The number rose to 164,004 in 1850 and reached a new high of 221,253 the following year. The number of German immigrants was 29,704 in 1840, 78,896 in 1850 and a high of 215,009 in 1854.[1] The Germans were roughly divided between Catholics, Protestants—Evangelical or Lutheran—and "free-thinkers."

Some immigrants chose to settle in the middle west. Most of those sailed directly to New Orleans and took a steamboat upriver to their destination. They met a varied reception, depending on the locality. Far more, especially the Irish, landed in the eastern seaboard cities and stayed there. Except for the railroad workers who moved along as they laid rails to the West, immigrant Catholics took little part in the westward movement, so vigorous at the time.

Unlike the Marylanders and other colonial Catholics of various nationalities, the newcoming Irish could not keep a low profile. They were alive in the activities of their parishes and in the Democrat politics of their precincts as soon as they became citizens. Many of them sought the same powers as trustees of their parishes as their Protestant neighbors enjoyed, and as Bishop John England was granting in the Carolinas. But other bishops and priests did not share the Carroll-England vision. A struggle for control ensued in many places.

Like their ancestors across the sea, the Irish in America often found working together difficult. Sometimes their opponents were fellow Hibernians. A dispute broke out between bishop and trustees, for instance, in St. Mary's Parish, the principal Catholic church in Philadelphia in the 1820s. The conflict continued during a 20-year period. At one time, a riot occurred during an election of trustees. Two factions of Irish parishioners, armed with clubs and bricks, acted as if they were facing Cromwell. The list of injured went over a hundred. Such rioting pointed the way for anti-foreign elements in the larger American population to turn on the Irish parishes later on. "They were ready to fight for their faith," a convert American writer said of them at the time, "but they didn't always understand it." Sometimes they fought each other.

And these Irish had a better start and an easier time than those who came as a result of the potato blight of the late 1840s. The vast majority of these "Famine Irish" had had little opportunity for education or training in skilled trades in their homeland. They crowded into run-down neighborhoods of large cities on the eastern seaboard and took menial and semi-skilled jobs. A carefree people, unaccustomed to possessions or care of them, they soon came into disrepute with the more established people of the area, sometimes even with those of their fellow Irish who had arrived earlier and now belonged to the middle class.

Some of these established Irish began to identify themselves socially with the Protestant majority. Even more, Irish Protestants, who had earlier worked with Catholics in the cause of freedom in Ireland, began to identify with Anglo-Americans in many cities rather than with their Irish compatriots who were Catholic. The newly-arrived Irish-Catholic abetted this split by identifying "Irish" with "Catholic." By this standard, to them no Protestant could be Irish even if the name were O'Fallon or McGuire and the birthplace Athlone or County Monaghan.

Before the Anglo-American majority accepted the newly-arrived Irish as "fellow Americans," some of the refugees of the famine began to identify themselves as "American" at the expense of immigrants from other countries, and occasionally even of American-born Catholics of another nationality. Recent arrivals in St. Patrick's Parish in St. Louis, for instance, asked Archbishop Peter Richard Kenrick, their Irish-born archbishop, to remove their "foreign" assistant pastor. He was a Missouri native, young Father Charles Ziegler, who spoke English with a Kentucky twang.

Archbishop Kenrick sent the Irish scurrying back to their "diggings" east of "Kerry Patch." Eventually Father Ziegler became the revered pastor of a prestigious Irish parish. But the archbishop had little success in stemming the tendencies of some Irish to look upon the non-Irish as foreigners or as non-Catholics. This was especially hard on the German-Catholics who faced triple jeopardy: the Irish Catholics criticized them because they were not Irish; Anglo-Americans rejected them because they were foreigners; the free-thinking and anti-clerical German immigrants (the so-called "Forty-Eighters" who left the German states after their failure to win freedom in 1848) rebuffed them because of their faith.

This ridiculous split between Irish and German Catholics caused a tremendous waste of energy in the Catholic community. Catholics needed a united front against the hostility that soon grew up around them. At the time immigration of Irish and German Catholics was approaching its zenith, the "common" or "public school" began to win widespread acceptance. Presumably neutral in religion, these schools generally reflected a Protestant ethos. Thus many tensions stemmed from school issues. The section on education will delve deeply into this sad story.

8

Trends in 19th Century American Education

Public education in America faced several options when it began in the second quarter of the last century. It might have followed the English system that considered education a private activity, with the government supporting and supplementing the private initiative, usually religious. Another possibility, the Prussian model, looked upon education as a state function, but recognized and supported various religious agencies, whether Lutheran, Catholic, or Evangelical Reformed, as proper sponsors of educational effort with children of their own members.

Indications pointed to a program for America's common or public schools similar to the program that England was to adopt or that was developing in Prussia. Education throughout the United States had been religious education with state financial aid available at times. Various denominations conducted their own parochial schools, academies and colleges.

Presumably the national and state government would continue to promote denominationally-based schools. Liberal presidents, such as James Monroe, accepted this principle of public aid in federal allotments. Most Protestant groups wanted parochial schools, but even those who did not support parochial education insisted that religion have a strong place in education.

Looking to the civic benefits of good education for all children in 1831, the town fathers of Lowell, Massachusetts began to consider how they could help the children of immigrant Irish parents. The Catholic parish had started a school, but it was small and limited in scope. The school board offered to rent the classrooms between nine o'clock and three o'clock daily from the Catholic parish, to hire and pay Catholic teachers, and defray the cost of utilities and insurance. The Church found the textbooks used in the public schools satisfactory and agreed to their use. The Church conducted religion classes before nine o'clock when the building was in its possession.

After a few years' trial, the school committee rated the program "eminently successful." By 1839, 752 children attended the Catholic-public school. It pointed a way that American education might have gone. Unfortunately, it did not.

Many factors played a part. All the English-speaking Protestant denominations accepted the King James version of the Bible. They understood toleration according to the law of William of Orange as acceptance of all forms of Protestantism. They were suspicious of dissent from the major Protestant tenets, either by Catholics or Mormons or any others of different religious traditions. The surge of Catholic immigration from Ireland and Germanic lands in the 30s and 40s brought this suspicious feeling to a boiling point, just at the time the "common" or public schools were coming into existence. Militant Protestants answered what they considered a Catholic threat to a Protestant country by two campaigns: one to control the growing public school movement; the other to stir hotheads all over the nation to attack Catholicism by voice, pen, club and fire.

In suburban Boston, on August 11, 1834, a mob stormed the Ursuline Sisters' Academy, patronized by the daughters of well-to-do Catholics and Unitarian families. After terrorizing the teachers and the students, mobsters destroyed the building. The courts refused to compensate the school, and Boston bigots honored the school-burners as American heroes.

Six years later, when Catholics in Philadelphia asked if Catholic children might use a different version of the Bible in public schools, and that the mandatory religious instruction be such as would square with their conscience, their fellow Philadelphians accused them of promoting "un-Christian education." A Protestant mob paraded through Catholic districts of Philadelphia, provoking and threatening. During the ensuing riot the mob burnt down the Catholic churches of St. Michael and St. Augustine. A grand jury blamed Catholics for provoking the rioters by attempting to protect their churches.

In that citadel of freedom, New York City, Catholics sought to discuss fair treatment for their children in the common schools, private in control, but supported by taxes. In response, nativists refused dialogue. They reached for clubs. They stormed the residence of Archbishop Hughes and rioted to deprive 20,000 Catholic youngsters, children of poor parents, of an education. The majority of the nativists had little regard for the rights of Jewish, Orthodox or Catholic minorities.

Even in St. Louis, usually tolerant since its French origin, violence broke out. Two groups of rioters threatened Catholic schools. A mob ransacked the St. Louis University College of Medicine in 1844 and another threatened the nun-teachers and forced the closing of the Sisters of St. Joseph's School for Blacks at Third and Poplar in the following year.[1] Nativist violence in Louisville resulted in the death of a dozen Catholic residents, recent immigrants from Germany and Ireland.

Even the system in Lowell, that had gotten off to such a good start, foundered. Minor disagreements probably would have worked themselves out in more normal times, such as the hiring of teachers who were not Catholic in repudiation of the inaugural agreement. In the tensions of the Know-Nothing period, minor disputes became mountains. The Lowell experiment ended in 1852. Within the 20 years of the Lowell plan's existence, the nation had moved from an attitude that saw education as a function of the various religious groups to a public school system separated from the churches of the American people. The public school began as an institution with a general Protestant outlook; it would become increasingly secularistic, especially in the urban environment.

Just as few American historians have looked into the ugly story of nativism, so few among the countless educational historians of competence have taken a hard look at some of the facts about the development of our public "nonsectarian" schools. One of the best of these few is Professor Lloyd R. Jorgenson of the

University of Missouri, Columbia. His June 1963 article in the *Phi Delta Kappan*, "Historical Origins of NonSectarian Public Schools, the Birth of a Tradition," has remained a classic statement on the subject,[2] even after his publication of an excellent book-length treatise *The State and the Non-Public Schools.*[2]

"Education," Professor Jorgenson insisted, "even under civil control, had a religious dimension, and the tradition of church-state cooperation in education . . . persisted."[3] When the common school movement got underway in the 1830s, it grew up as a distinctly Protestant phenomenon, with Protestant clergymen providing most of its leadership. In Kentucky, for instance, the first seven state superintendents (1838-1859) were ministers, the greatest of them, Robert Breckenridge, "a fiery anti-Catholic."[4]

When Catholics began to ask for an elimination of practices against the Catholic conscience, or a fair share of funds for their own "public" schools, the leaders of the Protestant groups—even those who had previously supported the idea of parochial schools—united to defend the public school. "In doing so," Jorgenson states, "they made explicit what they always assumed, that the public schools were Protestant institutions," and "the first line of defense against the growth of Catholicism."[5]

In New York City, a private philanthropic association, the Public School Society, controlled elementary education. Nominally nonsectarian, it used Protestant prayers and psalms, conducted Protestant religious instruction, required daily reading of the King James version of the Bible, criticized Catholics as "deceitful" and insulted the cherished beliefs and loyalties of the Catholic children, called the Pope a "man of sin, mystery of iniquity, son of perdition."[6] Even with the support of Governor William H. Seward, himself a Protestant, the Catholic parents could not get a fair hearing for their just demands.

Before 1835, only three states had laws prohibiting the use of public funds for parochial schools and in these states people openly disregarded the legislation. Michigan enacted such laws in 1835 and 21 states followed during the next three decades—almost all the states that had public educational programs.

By the last third of the century, these principles had common support: laws approved the reading of the Bible, with a large majority of state courts upholding these laws; and public funds would go only for "public" schools. These were nominally non-sectarian, but actually Protestant-oriented. The supporters of these two principles insisted on the use of the word "schools" rather than "education" so that state funds could still go to colleges and universities, most of them at the time under direct Protestant control.[7] The parochial school movement, once so strong among many Protestants—the Presbyterians had 250 at one time—came to be a negligible factor on the American scene, except among the Lutherans and Catholics.[8]

As the public school became interwoven with American life, many questioned the loyalty of those who did not attend. When Catholics complained about the Protestant orientation of the public schools, they were accused of being both "un-American" and "unChristian." Not getting their fair share of educational benefits, Catholics had to set up a distinct school system. Then their fellow Americans called them disloyal or divisive for doing so.

So antagonistic were Protestant militants to any legitimate concession to Catholic school children that slowly they came to support a public school system that became increasingly secularist in large cities, even though it remained generally Protestant Christian in small towns. Certainly Protestant leaders of the 1840s, Professor Jorgenson believed, would feel astounded at the secularist spirit of the urban public schools today.

The irony of the whole situation became clear only later. Professor Jorgenson concluded his article with these words: "It was a decisive victory for Protestants, but their doctrine of non-sectarianism was in time turned back against them. It was destined finally to destroy what they had originally sought to preserve—religious instruction in the public schools."[9]

Instead of giving a real free choice in education to those Catholics who were poor and could not afford other schools, the majority of Americans came to think they were doing the Catholics a favor by allowing them to build and maintain their own schools.

Catholics did not easily arrive at the decision to set up their own separate educational system. It was a dramatic step, an unprecedented sacrifice on the part of predominantly poor people and the countless dedicated religious women who for the most part staffed these schools. It should have brought acclaim from other deeply religious people. Instead, others viewed it first as unchristian, later on as separatist, divisive, un-American.

9

Catholic Beginnings in Higher Education

Two Catholic universities, Georgetown in the District of Columbia and St. Louis in Missouri, got under way in the early national period and established their regional reputations before other Catholic universities and, in fact, before many state institutions of their areas. Prominent bishops started these schools: John Carroll started Georgetown; Louis W.V. DuBourg, who had earlier been president of Georgetown, became Bishop of Louisiana Territory and opened a college in St. Louis. These bishops later invited Jesuits to staff the institutions.

Georgetown got under way in 1789, the same year that the national government did. Its creator, Bishop John Carroll, reflected the age of the founding fathers. He belonged to the southern "planter aristocracy," as did his cousin Charles Carroll, and three of our first four presidents. The Continental Congress, had in fact, sent him on an embassy to French Canada during the early years of the Revolution. Carroll's friend, President Washington, stopped by the school on one occasion to visit his two nephews, Bushrod and Augustine, who were students there. Washington invited the president of the college at the time, Father Louis W.V. DuBourg, to visit him at Mount Vernon. DuBourg accepted the invitation.

The College had the look of a Southern plantation with two rambling country school houses facing each other on a plateau above the Potomac River, just northwest of where the nation decided to build its national capitol. In spite of the monastic routine of study, chapel and general living, daily living at the school itself reflected the family life of the Southern manor house.

Neither at the outset nor later did the town and city of Washington have a high percentage of Catholic residents. As a result the school did not reflect the big-city, day-student ethos that so many Catholic universities were to do later on. It remained a residential school with heavy southern clientele. mainly from neighboring Maryland and distant Louisiana. Several times in its early history the absence of a large potential reserve of students in the neighborhood brought forth the recommendation that the school move to the expanding metropolitan center, New York City, with its growing Catholic population.

The school stayed in Washington, however, and its presence there gave it a national distinction and afforded its students an opportunity to go on special occasions to hear the great orators of the Congress: Clay, Webster and Calhoun. Future governors of North Carolina and of Maine went to Georgetown and the sons of Presidents John Tyler and Andrew Johnson. The former came to the commencement exercises in 1841, the latter was to come in 1869 when his successor, President U.S. Grant, presented the diplomas.

Like all American institutions that bore the name "college" before the Civil War, Georgetown had the aspect of a crack classical academy. Its students were in that age group. But the possibility of moving to a higher status was bright. The school's first big step came with the establishment of an astronomical observatory in 1841, a time when the country had only three such observatories, one at Williams College in Maine, one at Western Reserve in Ohio, and the Naval Observatory. "The subsequent research achievements of the observatory," historian Joseph T. Durkin, S.J., was to write, "comprise one of the great chapters in Georgetown's history."[1] Georgetown took a second step upward in 1843 when it gave birth to the first of several daughter institutions, Holy Cross College in Worcester, Massachusetts. The request of a group of prominent doctors to set up a medical school under the aegis of Georgetown University in

April 1851 marked the third step on the way to the status of a true university. These laymen-physicians were to work closely with the Jesuit-classicists, philosophers, and scientists over the years, and to remain loyal to the original scope of the school in a time of suggested change. During the Civil War, Georgetown suffered the physical and psychological stresses familiar only to the Border States, the nonseceding slave-holding areas. It survived, and took as its colors the blue and the gray, symbol of a reunited nation. Shortly after the conflict Georgetown opened a law school. Its future looked bright.

While those advances were taking place along the Potomac, Belgian Jesuits were breaking new ground in Missouri on a terrace above the Mississippi. The bishop of the Louisiana Territory, Louis W.V. DuBourg decided in 1819 to take up his residence in St. Louis rather than in New Orleans with its cathedral and established population. Among his many programs, he opened a college for boys in the metropolis of Territorial Missouri. The school had a checkered career in its early years. In 1828 Bishop DuBourg's successor, Bishop Joseph Rosati, C.M., invited Jesuit missionaries, then running a combined Indian school and seminary at Florissant, 20 miles from St. Louis, to staff St. Louis College.

In the second year of Jesuit direction, a Washington observer called St. Louis College (soon to win a charter as the first university west of the Mississippi) "the most flourishing college at this time in the United States."[2] St. Louis University began a medical school with a board of trustees composed by charter of representatives of each of the major religious denominations of the city. No school in the country at the time reflected such an ecumenical spirit. In the mid-40s it opened a school of law.

The most prominent citizens of the Trans-Mississippi Region, especially Louisiana and Missouri, sent their sons to St. Louis University, as did Spanish-speaking residents of Santa Fe, in the Republic of Mexico. Senator Thomas Hart Benton sought a federal land grant for the school in 1838, six years after the Congress had granted many city lots to Georgetown University. Besides graduating doctors, lawyers, businessmen, soldiers, government officials and explorers of the West, the University sent two of its alumni to the faculty of Harvard University in the days before the Civil War, Professor Ferdinand Bocher in Romance Languages, and Professor Lucien Carr in Anthropology.[4]

In 1840 a former president of St. Louis University accepted the invitation of Bishop John B. Purcell to take over a small college in Cincinnati. This was to be the first of many schools to grow out of St. Louis University. It took the name Xavier College. Others were Loyola of Chicago, Marquette in Milwaukee, Creighton in Omaha, and the University of Detroit. Until the middle of the following century, St. Louis would number among its alumni all presidents of Jesuit colleges throughout the middle west.

During the years Georgetown and St. Louis University were moving in their respective areas, Catholic colleges opened in many places: South Bend, Mobile, New York City, Boston, New Orleans, Providence, Pittsburg, Philadelphia, Chicago, Milwaukee, St. Paul, Dubuque, San Francisco, Santa Clara, Spokane, Newark, Grand Coteau, Louisiana and others. Highly-trained priests from Europe helped to set up these schools. Lay professor emigres joined them.

The bishops of the United States long considered the establishment of a central Catholic University with special emphasis on the advanced education of clerics. The long debates on the development of such an institution stemmed from the question of location or sponsorship. The great archdioceses of Baltimore and New York had strong reasons to support their claims; some bishops felt that the school should build on an existing institution such as Seton Hall College, while others thought it should be an entirely distinct institution. Arguments in favor of locating in Washington, D.C. had to overcome the belief of some that the presence in the national capitol might suggest too close a relationship with the government and might conflict with the already established Georgetown University in the neighborhood. Washington was finally to win out late in the century.

10

Roman Misjudgments

The two pontiffs who ruled during the second quarter of the 19th century rejected most of the aspirations of the time for freedom, equality and constitutional government. Leo XII alienated the many Catholics in Rome as well as the few Protestants and Jews. After the one-year pontificate of Pius VIII, the reactionary Pope Gregory XVI faced revolt in the Papal States. Only the might of the Austrian Army restored him to power. He responded with a police state.

When he died in 1846, most candidates for the papal chair reflected his repressive attitudes. They depended on Austrian strength, and rejected the aspirations of their own Italian people for independence and unity. In contrast with these, the cardinal who became Pope Pius IX seemed liberal. Actually he was an enlightened conservative, reflecting more the outlook of a "benevolent despot" of the previous century than that of a 19th-century president or prime minister. His public stance resembled that of King Charles III of Spain or King Gustavus III of Sweden of the previous century rather than that of his contemporaries Abraham Lincoln or William E. Gladstone.

His initial moves seemed to reflect the presumed liberalism. He put a civilian instead of a cleric in charge of the temporal affairs of the Papal States. He made agreements with Turkey over the holy places in Jerusalem and satisfactorily ended long negotiations with Russia, assuring a better situation for the Church in that empire. He granted some desired civil reforms but offered no comprehensive plan for improvement and drew up no constitution for the Papal States. Nonetheless, he enjoyed a year of popularity.

The Revolution of 1848 ended that. His fellow Italians wanted a united Italy, with Rome as its capital. That meant, first, the end of the Papal States, while the Pope looked on his temporal sovereignty as essential to the Papacy; and, secondly, it meant an attempt to expel the Austrians who controlled much of the peninsula while the Pope could not, as spiritual head of all Catholics, take part in a war against the Austrian Empire, a country with a large Catholic population. The Austrian armies put down the revolt, and restored the earlier arrangements. During the next 20 years Pius IX was to remain in an independent papal territory only with the help of foreign forces, who protected his earthly authority against the hopes of his own people.

Historians had called Pius IX's predecessors reactionary. With him historians added the word "maladroit."[1] His predecessors had condemned many modern beliefs they thought wrong. Seeing little good in modern trends, Pius IX was to condemn almost every cherished belief of people in the free world. Sickly in youth, he was highly emotional. Superficially educated, he considered an honest disagreement a personal affront. Surrounded by intransigents, he reflected their rigidity. Yet withal a good and pious man, a concerned pastor, a man of simplicity, he won from the common people of the world a personal regard that his successors to the present time continue to enjoy. Many Catholics hoped for his canonization.

Pius IX was the first pope to have a great deal to do with America. His first action turned out to be a blunder. Deciding to send a special delegate to the States in 1853, he chose as his representative an Italian, Archbishop Gaetano Bedini, who had been associated with the reactionary rule of the Papal States. His position had depended on the Austrian Army that had put down the Italian struggle for independence. That army then took part in the suppression of the fight for liberty throughout the Hapsburg Empire.

As a result of these abortive struggles for freedom and constitutional government, many Italians, Hungarians, and German revolutionaries had fled to the United States. They brought with them an intense hatred of the Catholic faith and the Austrian Empire. Americans welcomed them as fellow fighters for freedom. Nativists who normally resented both foreigners and Catholics, but hated "papists" more, joined in the welcome. These "nativists" had formed a "Know-Nothing" Party and began asserting themselves in the 1852 election, electing their own candidates and rioting to keep Catholics from the polls. This hostile climate faced the Pope's delegate.

The Pope might more wisely have designated an American churchman, such as Archbishop Francis Patrick Kenrick of Baltimore, as his representative. He had already named Archbishop Paul Cullen of Armagh apostolic delegate to Ireland. Cullen would have been an acceptable alternative, as would others, Archbishop William Walsh of Halifax, for instance. Both these men knew the language and shared the ancestral background of many of America's bishops and people. But the Pope sent Bedini.

The Italian Archbishop arrived in June 1853, allegedly on his way to serve as papal nuncio to the Emperor of Brazil. He went to Washington where President Franklin Pierce greeted him courteously. But segments of the press saw in this interview an attempt to set up diplomatic relations between Rome and Washington. Demonstrators and rioters began to threaten Bedini as he moved west to Pittsburg, Cincinnati and Louisville. An Italian revolutionary society considered assassinating him. He curtailed his visit and slipped out of New York harbor secretly during the winter. Archbishop Peter Richard Kenrick of St. Louis, brother of the Baltimore prelate, called the visit "a collection of blunders."[2] Kenrick was probably correct, also, in his earlier surmise that the Nuncio's visit had one purpose in appearance and another in actuality.[3] Instead of going to Brazil as he allegedly intended to do, Bedini returned to Rome, where the Pope later named him a cardinal.

The Pope's second major mistake put American Catholics on the defensive for a century and a quarter, and gave sincere Protestants ample justification, almost a mandate, to fight the excessive growth of Catholicism. Instead of acknowledging that the United States remained one of the few places where Catholics could enjoy rational freedom and protection of their persons and property, Rome launched a *Syllabus of Errors* that apparently condemned many cherished American beliefs.

These condemnations, drawn up by a commission of cardinals and issued by Pope Pius IX in 1864, included ideas worthy of condemnation as well as attitudes Americans revered. Many of the anathemas, further, had appeared in documents that dealt with specific situations in European localities. The manner of presentation seemed to suggest that they applied to the universal Church. The wording often meant one thing to churchmen in Naples, Italy, and another to people in Naples, Florida. This confusion argued against its promulgation in the New World. But Rome saw it otherwise.

Some of the propositions, such as those numbered 47 to 55, made sense everywhere and at all times. They simply asked all countries to do what the First Amendment required of the American government, namely to stay out of purely internal church affairs, such as the appointing and deposing of bishops and setting rules for religious profession. Interestingly, while Rome was always ready to clamp down on Americans, it continued to allow rulers in Latin countries and anticlerical French premiers to influence the choice of bishops and allowed the Austrian monarch to have a negative hand in the choice of Pope. (Austria no longer has a monarch; but France has a premier who recently held up the appointment of a coadjutor archbishop.)

While these few propositions had universal validity, many others flew in the face of cherished beliefs of Americans. Some even offended good sense. Upon reading them, St. Thomas of Aquin might well have thought church leadership had repudiated reason. One of the most severe was the 80th proposition that said a Catholic was "anathema," that is "cursed" or "excommunicated," if he or she held that the Church should or could "reconcile itself with progress, liberalism and modern civilization." Americans felt that their country represented the best in liberalism, and in progress, and while not as advanced materially, commercially and industrially as Britain at the time, still was well on the way to becoming a "modern, civilized" country.

Another anathema faced American Catholics with the realization that they had to hold that the Catholic religion should be the only religion of this state to the exclusion of all others. In countries predominantly Catholic, rulers had to refuse immigrants, even refugees, permission to worship publicly according to their own beliefs. They could not allow liberty of worship or public expression of opinion. They had to accept "union of Church and State"—a sorry set-up that had brought endless troubles to the Church in so many countries.

This last theory set back full acceptance of the Church in America for a hundred years. It was a proposition untenable rationally and made it imperative for sincere Protestants to work against any situation that might give Catholics political power in America. It proved a continual embarrassment to American Catholics who asked of the Protestant majority what their Church would not accord to their Protestant neighbors in any place where Catholics were the majority. Catholic apologists from Robert Bakewell, editor of the *Shepherd of the Valley*, the Catholic paper in St. Louis, to the editors of leading Catholic weeklies on the Atlantic seaboard, wasted much of their time trying to justify this strange political view.[4]

This theory would seem to give to political leaders the capacity to make a religious decision. Rome never explained what gave Czar Alexander III of Russia or Kaiser Wilhelm I of Germany, or even "good old" Franz Joseph of Austria the capacity to make religious decisions. Yet that is what the Church was saying: that these rulers should recognize the Catholic Church as the only true Church—a religious not political decision. If Franz Joseph decided that his Catholic Church was correct and restricted Protestants, what kept Kaiser Wilhelm I from favoring his fellow Protestants and applauding his Chancellor Bismark's persecution of Catholics? And wouldn't the Church have to approve Czar Alexander III's restrictions on all but Orthodox?

Had not the Church in its very beginning fought the notion of a state-dominated religion when its martyrs defied Nero, Decius and Diocletian, all-powerful emperors? The popes made reluctant concessions to King Francis I of France in the 16th century, lest he try to establish an independent state-church as his neighbor in England, Henry VIII, was doing. The "Eldest Daughter of the Church," as France liked to call herself, responded with an independent spirit called "Gallicanism" that tended to ignore papal authority in most matters, giving overwhelming authority to bishops and councils.

After several centuries this reluctant concession to the French King and other monarchs became almost a dogma of faith. Rome seemed to ignore the fact that it was succumbing in practice to a theory it had rejected in the 16th century when expressed by Germans in the Latin formula *Cujus regio, illius est religio,* literally "whose is the region, his is the religion." In short, the ruler could determine the religion of his subjects. What was a reluctant concession to several kings in the 1500s had become a sanctified Catholic teaching in the 1800s.

All rulers of all times presumed to decide religious questions until the founding Fathers of America said, not simply out of pure speculative wisdom, but for many practical reasons of course, "religion is not government's sphere."

11

Catholics and the Civil War

The Civil War gave new heroes to the nation: Lincoln and Grant in the North and Lee and Davis to the South. Interest in the conflict brings hundreds of thousands to the battlefields, especially Gettysburg. It is almost a mystical experience for some. The Civil War provided the setting for Hollywood's most popular movie "Gone With The Wind." The conflict retains a compelling interest seemingly going beyond reason at times.

All these glamorous memories detract from the central fact: the War Between the States marked one major breakdown in the American system. At one time in its history, debate, discussion and compromise could not solve the problems facing the nation. Extremists split the Democratic Party, allowing the Republican Party in the Northeast to elect a minority president, Abraham Lincoln. States of the deep South felt that they could no longer get a fair deal within the Union and seceded. Then they blundered into firing on the flag over Fort Sumter.

From the vantage of the late 20th century, the issues of 1861 seem simple and straightforward: union or disunion, slavery or freedom. But the issues did not seem so clear-cut at the time or at other times since then. In the North many were willing to fight for the Union. They did not want to see the land broken into many rival sections with regular bloody struggles such as had plagued the European continent. Many, too, wanted to bring an end to the existence of slavery, but they had no suggestion as to what to do with the Blacks once they were free.

Abolitionists, such as the late John Brown, thought slavery should be destroyed by any means.

Residents of the Border States, such as Kentucky and Missouri, thought of their areas as buffer territory. Hundreds hoped to set up a safety belt that would prevent northern invasion of the South or southern raids into the North. Many of their neighbors just north of the Ohio River believed that the government should not coerce their brothers in the South. Still others believed that the struggle would end in a stalemate. The only sound conclusion, they thought, was to call off hostilities.

Archbishop Peter Richard Kenrick of St. Louis, who believed in the absolute separation of church and state functions, held a position of Olympian neutrality over a divided flock. As the war went on, and arbitrary rule, military and civilian, dominated his city, the wisdom of this policy became clear. Some priests in Maryland refused to follow their acting bishop's directive of praying for the success of the Union armies. The Border States, in short, shared all manner of opinion on the War.

Just as the North had its John Brown, the South had its extremists, too, fire eaters who wanted to get out of the Union at any cost and some who were willing to stay in only if the government fought the English Navy to reopen the slave trade. But these were a minority. The average Southerner was a family-farmer who owned a small plot and no slaves. But he did accept slavery as a reality of his area and the slave owners as his political leaders. And he loved his home state and did not want "Yankees"—to him New England abolitionists—telling him what to do.

Free blacks loved the area, too. When the war broke out, a group of free "men of color" took up arms and marched out to defend Louisiana, as their ancestors had done under the leadership of Andrew Jackson against the British in 1815. The sovereign state of Mississippi refused to allow them to cross its borders.

Many Southerners, and a few eminent historians in both areas, shared the view of Father John B. Bannon. This most noted Confederate chaplain of the trans-Mississippi looked upon the war as a struggle against the overwhelming economic power of northern businessmen who wanted to treat the South as a "colony" in the way the British Empire treated its crown colonies like Jamaica or like Father Bannon's native Ireland; in short, it was a struggle provoked by northern economic imperialism.

Few individuals did more to foster the heroic tradition of the South after the war than Father Abram Ryan with his heartwarming ballads "The Conquered Banner," and "The Sword of Robert Lee." The North also had its Irish Catholic balladeer, the noted bandleader Patrick Sarsfield Gilmore, who composed the popular war song "When Johnny Comes Marching Home," and whose "Matchless Band" literally had no match in the years after the struggle.

The American superior of a religious order of men, which began before the religious division of Western Europe, called attention to an ancient rule of his founder that forbade public discussion of "conflicts between Christian princes." He urged his members to accept the de facto government in their respective areas and pointed to the special problems of the border cities where so many of his fellow religious worked. Interestingly, he saw no compelling moral issue in the struggle.[1]

The majority of Catholics, north and south, reflected the views of their states. The list of heroes on both sides included Catholics: Generals Sheridan and Rosecrans with the Union; General Beauregard and Admiral Semmes with the Confederates. The Catholic community had even more heroic individuals off the battlefield: 640 of the 3200 Civil War nurses, according to reliable estimates, were nuns from 20 separate communities representing 12 distinct congregations.[2]

Nuns were almost the only trained nurses in America at the outbreak of the war and among the few who had battlefield experience. The Mercy Superior, Mother Teresa Maher, and several of her associates, had nursed wounded soldiers during the Crimean War in 1854 before coming to America. An attitude had prevailed in both North and South before the war that a woman compromised her reputation by nursing outside her home. The total incapacity of Scarlett O'Hara to handle wartime hospital situations in the novel and movie "Gone With The

Wind" reflected the experience of middle-class American wom-
ankind. It was not the picture of an individual alone.

Outside their own hospitals, nuns such as Sister Angela
Heath, a Daughter of Charity, found conditions deplorable, both
in the poorly-equipped and unsanitary field hospitals and in the
dismal quarters provided for the nuns. The nuns came into military health service in various ways: some by the call of their
state governors, some by volunteering to their states, and still
others by turning over their hospitals for military use and continuing to staff them.

The prejudice against Catholic sisterhoods, stirred by Calvinist preachers in New England towns and the rural South and
Midwest, made their charitable efforts often initially resisted.
They faced continual ridicule because of their presumed beliefs
and their choice of garb.[4] This hostile attitude of some common
soldiers on both sides made many question the much vaunted
tolerance of American men. Ignorance may have explained the
hostility in part. But historians would have expected at least
professional respect on the part of Dorothea Dix, Director of
Nurses for the North. Her biographer, Helen Marshall, however, stated clearly that she discriminated against the nun-
nurses because of their religion.[5]

Typical of Miss Dix's directives was her removal of the Sisters of Charity from Camp Dennison even though the officers
and men of the Tenth (Ohio) Regiment wanted them to stay.[6]
After consistent complaints, especially from physicians who had
worked at nuns' hospitals before the war, the Assistant Surgeon
General, E.D. Townsend, at the request of Edwin Stanton,
Federal Secretary of War, curbed Dorothea Dix's power in October 1863.

Dorothea Dix performed valuable service to her country in
the area of prison reform, and rightly deserves her reputation
as an American heroine. Her Civil War work, even beyond her
treatment of the nun-nurses, failed to match her earlier effort.
She simply did not understand these other American heroines
or appreciate their religious dedication.

An even greater injustice, totally inexcusable, has continued
over the years. Historian after historian of the Civil War period,

in both major surveys and in sectional studies, have omitted the nuns' great contribution to the welfare of the ill and wounded soldiers on both sides. A 10-volume photographic history of the war, by way of example, published in 1911 when many veterans of hospitals still lived, devoted 140 pages, with at least one illustration on each page, without mentioning, much less picturing, a single nun-nurse.[7] To make amends in part for the failure of his fellow historians, the distinguished octogenarian scholar John Tracy Ellis pointed out that this generous service of so many dedicated religious women was "one of the most inspiring—and little known—chapters of the Civil War."[8]

The draft laws did not give "equal protection." In the South the planter could stay at home if he had twenty slaves on his spread; in the North anyone who could pay a substitute $300 was exempt. In northern cities the established Anglo-Americans generally were in a better economic position than the recent immigrants, many of whom were Irish Catholics. Thus the two groups whose economic interests had their part in bringing on the war could stay at home while poor men, farmers in the South and farmers and unskilled workers in the North, fought the battles. At least one businessman in the North, in fact, frankly expressed the hope that his sons were not so stupid as to succumb to recruiting propaganda.

When the federal draft came in 1863, many justices, especially those in Wisconsin, thought it unconstitutional. The Governor of New York criticized it sharply in a July 4th address. Shortly after the long list of Irish casualties at Gettysburg was reported, the New York draft board set up unjust quotas that called up Irish in disproportionate numbers.

At the same time, dock workers, many of them Irish Catholics, found their long hours and poor pay not too far above slavery, and went on strike. The employers brought in blacks as scabs. While modern legislation limits strike-breaking today, employers had no restrictions then. Further, the police looked to the protection of property, not to the interests of the workers.

With employers pitting one oppressed group (the black strike-breakers) against another oppressed group (the Irish workers subject to unfair draft arrangements), one should not be surprised that the latter turned on the former. And while one should not excuse the latter group, one should not overlook the grave fault of the employers. When the white dock-workers turned on the black strike-breakers, the police, also in great part Irish, tried to stop the attackers. The ensuing riots, with many black victims, lasted for four days. Eventually Archbishop John Hughes and many priests of the neighborhood succeeded in calming the rioters. It was a sad day in the history of the New York Irish. It would take another major war to bring a fair draft law; and even longer for the law to limit the use of strike-breakers by unethical and unconcerned employers.

After Gettysburg, the Army of the Potomac rested for the remainder of the year. But in 1864, Grant moved relentlessly toward Richmond even though he lost more men than Lee had in his whole army. In the meantime, Confederate President Jefferson Davis sent Father John Bannon, former Missouri pastor and Confederate chaplain, as special envoy to Ireland. Bannon had great success in convincing those Irish, who thought of going to the States, to stay home for the duration.

The war had split more than the country. It had divided many of the Protestant denominations into sections. In certain areas of the border states, such as out-state Missouri, even after the end of the war, many Southern ministers were bush-wacked. Many of the religious divisions endured for a long time. The Catholics, on the other hand, remained united.

A year after the war ended, the bishops of the country gathered in Baltimore for a national council. The mere fact of the meeting of a still united hierarchy left an impression reflected magnificently some years later by Bishop John Lancaster Spalding of Peoria, in a life of his uncle, Archbishop Martin Spalding of Baltimore, who presided at the gathering. It bears quotation at length:

> The country had just come forth from a terrible crisis
> ... Brother's hand had been raised against brother.
> ... The sects had been torn asunder and still lay in
> disorder and confusion.
>
> Half of the country was waste and desolate; the people crushed, bowed beneath the double weight of

memory of the past . . . and the thought of a future which seemed hopeless.

On the other side there were weariness and exhaustion which follows a supreme effort, and the longing for peace and happiness after so much bloodshed and misery.

All were ready to applaud any power that had been able to live through that fateful struggle unhurt and unharmed; and when the Catholic Church walked forth before the eyes of the nation, clothed in the panoply of undiminished strength and of unbroken unity, thousands who but a while ago would have witnessed this manifestation of a power with jealous concern now hailed it with light as a harbor of good omen.[9]

The Council should have done much more, especially with plans to incorporate better the black Catholics and to welcome other blacks who might want to join the Church. Archbishop Martin Spalding looked upon emancipation as offering a golden opportunity. Few bishops shared his vision. Archbishop P.R. Kenrick of St. Louis felt that the bishops had done all they could. None looked to new approaches. The assembled bishops felt they had a more immediate responsibility for young white Catholics growing up in the large cities of the nation where the families scarcely had "the light, and space and air" they needed.

While admitting the limitations, historians must give praise to this meeting of the bishops, a gathering of men who only a short time before had stood with their own people in a sectional war. By their peaceful gathering, they showed that they had not let that struggle wipe out their sense of Catholic Christian unity.

12

The Impact of Converts

The addition of four distinguished Anglo-Americans to the Catholic community by way of conversion at mid-century helped to counteract the nativistic charge that Catholics were European immigrants. The four, in order of admission to the Church, were a Kentucky physician, a Universalist preacher, a young idealist and a Protestant Episcopal Bishop.

As important as these four men were, however, they did not have the tremendous human interest as the earlier conversion of one entire family, the Barbers. They came in *en masse*, father, mother, grandfather, and five children. Reverend Daniel Barber, the grandfather, had served in the Continental Army during the American Revolution before becoming an Episcopal minister. When a member of his parish posed a question on the Anglican succession, he referred the matter to his son, Reverend Virgil Barber, pastor of St. John's Episcopal Church in Waterbury, Connecticut. As a result of this study, the younger Barber became convinced of the truth of the Catholic faith and entered the Church in 1816. His father followed him and wrote books on Catholic teaching.

Within six years, Virgil Barber felt a call to the Jesuit priesthood. Six obstacles stood in the way: his wife, Jerusha, their son and four daughters, the youngest, Jane, only two years of age. Jerusha came to see the hand of God in her husband's call and applied to enter the Visitation Convent at Georgetown, D.C. She enrolled Jane in the Visitation Nursery School.

The pain of separation proved almost overwhelming for both husband and wife in early years, but gradually they were able to find peace of soul. Virgil Barber did pastoral and missionary work in upper New England and taught Hebrew at the Jesuit colleges at Georgetown and Frederick, MD. The son, Samuel, followed his father into the Jesuits, was Master of Novices at Frederick, Maryland, Rector in Washington, and Professor of French at Georgetown College. The three older girls joined the Ursuline Sisters in Quebec. Jane, the youngest, on reaching maturity, followed her mother into the Visitation.

As Sister Josephine, Jane Barber went with a pioneering team of sisters who opened Menard Academy on the Illinois frontier in 1834. Her mother followed two years later and proved a supportive "big sister" for her daughter and the other young nun educators. Sister Josephine wrote a history of her school and her family. At her death in the late 1880s, the newspaper in St. Louis, where she taught during her late years, acclaimed her as "famous in the annals of the Catholic Church in America."[1] She had taught many distinguished ladies, including Mrs. Winfield Scott Hancock, wife of the famous general, who, had the votes in one or two more states gone to her husband in the presidential election of 1880, would have been first lady of the land during Sister Josephine's late years.

Moses Linton, native of Nelson County, Kentucky, a Catholic enclave near the once-episcopal see of Bardstown, studied medicine under a Catholic physician at Transylvania College (later the University of Kentucky). He continued his medical education in Paris. After returning from France in 1840 at the age of 28, he entered the Catholic Church.

Linton's conversion so shook the Protestant populace of the Trans-Allegheny region, that a prominent minister, the Reverend Robert Grundy, felt the move demanded a response. He published a pamphlet attacking Dr. Linton for his rejection of Bible Christianity. Linton defended his decision with strength, good manners, and a pleasing style of written English.

Dr. Linton joined the faculty of medicine at St. Louis University when it began during the school year 1842-43. He taught gynecology, obstetrics and pediatrics and edited the *Saint Louis*

Medical and Surgical Journal. For many years it was the only medical and surgical journal published west of the Alleghenies.

On Washington's birthday in 1844 a nativist mob, inflamed by wild rumors, ransacked the building of the St. Louis University Medical School and destroyed all the equipment. Dr. Linton defended his school in a public address that soon merited publication. In words reminiscent of those of his fellow Kentuckian Abraham Lincoln, given 20 years later, Linton urged his fellow Catholics to take a long view. "I, for one," he stated "have too much confidence in the good sense and honesty of my countrymen to be long influenced by a prejudice so unreasonable."[2]

In the year 1845 Father John Timon, Superior of the Vincentian Fathers, and later Bishop of Buffalo, addressed a group of St. Louis laymen on the new association formed in France by Frederick Ozanam. Completely convinced of the validity of Ozanam's program, these laymen sought the permission of Bishop Peter Richard Kenrick to set up the first unit of the St. Vincent de Paul Society in America. They chose Dr. Linton as their first president.

Dr. Linton distinguished himself on two other occasions: as physician during the cholera epidemic that swept away one out of every ten St. Louisans in 1849; and as constitutionalist during the Reconstruction Days at the end of the Civil War. A strong Unionist and antislavery advocate, Linton supported an aggressive pursuit of victory, but a moderate, not a vindictive, peace. While most of the moderate Unionists served with Sherman's army, a group of "Radical Republicans" took control of domestic politics. They had wanted to oust Lincoln. When he died, they worked for a vindictive peace with a restrictive constitution, and an oath to take the vote from their opponents.

Under the leadership of Charles Drake, a native of Cincinnati who practiced law in St. Louis, they took control of the Missouri Constitutional Convention of 1865. Linton, the only Catholic in the group, led the moderates. Realizing that a frontal attack would gain nothing, he resorted to humorous verse that brought laughs at the expense of "Drake and his ducklings." In spite of Linton's best efforts, however, the constitution passed, only to be replaced a few years later. The Church of St.

Louis memorialized Dr. Linton's career with a mosaic of him in the "Great Cathedral."

Levi Silliman Ives (1797-1867), a native of upstate New York, became Protestant Episcopal Bishop of North Carolina in 1831. Fourteen years later he founded the Brotherhood of the Holy Cross whose views reflected those of the Oxford Movement in England. But members of his denomination pressured him to disband the Brotherhood and reject Catholic tendencies. He did so, but in 1852, he went to Rome and formally submitted to Pope Pius IX.

The conversion of this first bishop since the Reformation offered an unprecedented opportunity to the Church. Only one suggestion was forthcoming: that he be ordained a deacon and made Vicar Apostolic of North Carolina. That suggestion did not carry to fruition. Ives had given up more than his position in the Episcopalian Church. He had lost the means of livelihood for himself and his wife who followed him into the Church.

Only later in New York did he find a second career in Catholic charities. His home at the time became a meeting place for those who wished to discuss religious matters.

Orestes Brownson grew up in a Methodist milieu in his native Vermont, switched to Presbyterianism, preached Universalism and moved later into agnosticism. By advocating radical social causes as a writer and editor, he came to the attention of many advanced thinkers. He became a friend of Emerson and others in his circle. He spent some time at Brook Farm in Massachusetts, a place where thoughts grew more profusely than crops. There idealists lived plainly and thought profoundly.

Brownson broke with old friends at the age of 41 in 1844 and entered the Catholic Church. As editor of *Brownson's Quarterly Review*, he brought an entirely fresh voice and unexpected attitude to the Catholic community. A man of penetrating intellect and vigorous and lucid style, he wrote in a militant tone on religion, philosophy, literature, politics, what-have-you. He opposed a wide range of attitudes in the Catholic community he had entered: the hesitancy to speak out on the basic moral issue of slavery, the outmoded methods of education that he saw in some Catholic schools, and the tendency of Catholics to withdraw from the American mainstream into their own national precincts. He stressed the church's constant need of renewal.

He criticized Jesuit viewpoints often. But 100 years later, midwestern Jesuits singled out his acute appraisal of their early years under Belgian apostolic-oriented leadership in contrast to the more monastic attitudes of eastern Jesuits.[3] At first he took liberal views; but after the *Syllabus of Errors* in 1864 he turned conservative.

The prestige the Church enjoyed from the presence of such a distinguished spokesman among its members far outweighed the influence of the guidance he gave on any specific issue.

Isaac Hecker, a charismatic leader with a warm personality, obvious sincerity and frank manner, also spent time at Brook Farm and later came into the Church. He left a far greater legacy: the Congregation of St. Paul, a body of men dedicated to making converts, preaching in effective, current English, writing and lecturing on the topics of the day, and publishing a highly literate journal, the *Catholic World*, that combined solid learning with pleasant style, and many excellent books.

But Hecker did not move from his friends Emerson and Thoreau to the founding of a new congregation by a straight path. He looked into various forms of Protestantism. He came under Brownson's influence. After his conversion he joined the Redemptorists. A few years later, he tried to get his brother priests, many of them immigrants from Germany, to adjust more noticeably to American ways and went to Rome to bring this about. Expelled from the congregation, he appealed to Rome. Released from the Redemptorists, he launched out in a new direction.

Many of his early followers were also converts, men who had grown up and received their education in the Anglo-American Protestant milieu. Better educated than most priests, the Paulists were ready to try new phrasing of traditional theological expressions and to use new techniques in spreading Catholic truths. At a time when the majority of Catholic clergy never saw the inside of a Protestant church, Paulists would on appropriate occasions accept invitations to occupy the pulpit of another denomination. Hecker left his followers with clear-cut goals and an ecumenical spirit rare at the time.

Over the years, many other prominent converts were to enrich the life of the American Catholic community. Among these were General William Rosecrans and his brother, Sylvester, Bishop of Columbus. Several converts came from families distinguished in public life, Archbishop James Roosevelt Bayley in the 19th century and Avery Dulles in the 20th. The lives of many of these could be discussed with equal claim.

13

Vatican I— A Missed Opportunity

Just as Americans do not want to look on the Civil War as the terrible calamity that it was, so few Catholics have recognized the First Vatican Council of 1870 as the failure that it was. Yet in one major way it failed. The Church had lost the mind of Europe. In the *Syllabus of Errors* a few years before, Pope Pius IX had talked about the many problems the Church faced. It needed new directions and a fresh spirit.

The Church's three-centuries-old reliance on the "Most Christian King" and "His Catholic Majesty," as popes called the Bourbon Kings of France and Spain, had brought disaster. The Church had blessed the thrones and supported those who sat on them. Now the rulers of the traditionally Catholic countries had turned on the Church. They closed seminaries, confiscated colleges and expelled priests, nuns, and brothers. The Chancellor of Prussia, Otto von Bismarck, was about to seduce the pretentious emperor of the French, Napoleon III, into declaring war against a poised and overpowering Prussian military force. Bismarck had used Napoleon III's blindness to weave his web around the Catholic provinces of west and south Germany. Within five years he would openly persecute Catholics and restrict the freedom of the Church.

Italy and Spain had thrown out capable priests who found freedom and opportunity to exercise their priestly zeal in the New World. Piedmontese troops encamped a short distance from Rome, ready to seize the remaining section of the papal states once Napoleon III fell into Bismarck's trap.

Catholic Poland groaned under Czarist tyranny. Ireland had scarcely survived the long years of potato blight and still languished under British tyranny. Millions of European Catholics had fled across the sea to America, the land of freedom and opportunity. Millions more would soon follow. There they were finding a chance to build a new life, if not for themselves, at least for their descendants. The government confiscated no churches, jailed no priests, closed no colleges. American archbishops, such as the Dean among them, John Baptist Purcell of Cincinnati, pointed out the greatness of the system that the American people had developed.

With the Church going down in Europe and having found an opening in America, one would have expected the churchmen of the Old World to look gratefully to the New and to have asked what had brought the better situation overseas. They should have welcomed the Americans as heralds of a new dispensation. Instead they scarcely gave the U.S. bishops a decent hearing.

The dictatorial procedures made many critics wonder if enough freedom existed to constitute a real council. The American bishops, led by Peter Richard Kenrick of St. Louis, along with bishops of many countries, wondered why they could not elect the members of the committee that made up the rules. Why had the conciliar commissions been chosen before the Fathers of the Council had a chance to meet these men and know their qualifications for their important posts? Why was the time-honored right of Council members to introduce proposals no longer in vogue? With the agenda so concerned with European problems that brought only European answers already tried and found wanting over many decades, could it really be called a *universal* council? Was the about-to-die Papal States of more consequence than the hundreds of thousands of Catholics in Africa, Asia and the Americas?

Bishop Augustin Verot of Savanna, Georgia, thought not. A scientist as well as a theologian, he asked for a statement of reconciliation between the Church and modern science. He urged the Council Fathers to recognize the good faith of those who did not belong to the Catholic Church. And, as one who had long witnessed what slavery and racism meant, he asked affirmation of the unity and common humanity of colored and white races. Such a declaration was far more important, he pointed out, than discussing the complicated theories of obscure German philosophers.

This last remark of Bishop Verot about the Teutonic think-tank recalled a pre-conciliar report of theologian James A. Corcoran, a priest of Charleston, South Carolina. He had written it two years before when he was a member of the commission that dealt with doctrinal matters in preparation for the Council. Corcoran complained that the Fathers planned too many definitions "often because some Professor Scratzkenback in some German university has written about them in a German philosophical jargon which neither himself nor his readers understand."[1] Even though educated in Rome and familiar with Roman ways, Corcoran had found the procedures and the mania for secrecy totally irksome.[2]

The best statement of what the Council should have heeded was the recommendation of Archbishop John Baptist Purcell of Cincinnati: "Our civil constitution grants perfect liberty to every denomination of Christians . . . I verily believe this was infinitely better for the Catholic religion, than were it the special object of the state's patronage and protection . . . All we want is a free field and no favor. Truth is mighty and will prevail."[3]

In spite of this great opportunity for the church to open its mind and heart to its newest section that was pointing the way the world was turning, the controlling Fathers of the Council decided to keep the outmoded ways, to continue the alliance with monarchs whose days were done, to oppose "liberty and modern civilization," to condemn obscure German philosophers whose theories no one understood or cared about and to ignore the existence of racists who denied the unity of humankind to promote "white supremacy."

Bishop Bernard McQuaid of Rochester, New York, wrote at the time: "If I had not confidence in God's protecting hand, I would run from the Council in despair, so strangely ignorant are many men of what is going on in the world."[4] At that time the question of infallibility had not come up. On that subject, McQuaid wrote, "The ablest bishops by far that have spoken in the Council are bishops whose views are known to be adverse to any definition."[5]

Under pressure of a beleaguered Pontiff and the adroit politicking of an English cardinal, the Fathers promoted a theory of papal infallibility that 39 of the 49 American bishops felt at least inopportune. Eight of these ten supporters of a definition were French-Americans from New England, the Pacific Northwest and the Gulf states.

One of these, the French-born bishop of Natchitoches, Louisiana, Augustus M. Martin, saw the entire issue in a totally French context with the supporters of the Pope battling against "the old Gallicanism, modern rationalism and a wicked spirit of independence."[6] All the while "the immense majority of the clergy and faithful," he insisted, "has been calling for a Definition of the Dogma of Infallibility."[7] Most observers concluded that this "immense majority" existed only in the minds of the editors of the Jesuit journal *Civilta Cattolica*.

Some American prelates simply did not hold that the Pope could speak infallibly without the consent of the bishops. Others hesitated to pronounce on the issue itself, and simply insisted that a definition at that time was inopportune. One of the stiffest opponents of the definition in the mind of several European historians, Archbishop Peter Richard Kenrick of St. Louis, saw no compelling reason for the definition in scripture or tradition.[8] In general, those countries with large Protestant populations, such as England, Germany, Canada and the United States, and those with Orthodox neighbors, saw only added difficulties in ecumenical discussions with their fellow Christians of other denominations. The French hierarchy was split. The majority of bishops from Belgium, Holland and Portugal presumably were against the declaration.

A prominent theologian of the Greek Orthodox Church, Sergius Bulgakov, wrote a short book condemning the declaration of Vatican I with a significant argument. If the vote had been taken by countries, he suggested, it would have been overwhelmingly defeated.[9] The vast majority of the more than 500 bishops who voted for infallibility were from Italy and Spain; most of them, further, supported the definition not on sound theological or historical grounds, but presumably because, with the gradual destruction of the Papal States, the Papacy needed a different kind of support.

When the final vote was tallied on July 18, 1870, twenty-five Americans voted yes. Edward Fitzgerald of Little Rock was one of two bishops who voted no in the final tally. The remaining American bishops, including Peter Richard Kenrick and Augustin Verot, had already departed Rome. The former was scolded by a self-appointed committee of European bishops during the next few years. This harassment took place even though Kenrick openly admitted on his return to St. Louis that he accepted the decrees of the Council.

The Church had lost a great opportunity and would move into the 20th century in 19th-century horse-drawn carriages.

14

Catholic Parochial Schools Take Root Slowly

Many German immigrants arrived in a better financial situation than the famished and destitute Irish. When the Germans began their parochial schools, they met little resistance from the general Anglo-American community. Several factors brought this about. Many German parochial schools began in country towns, some totally Germanic in population. All functioned in a German-speaking community. They did not disturb native American sensitivities in urban areas. The Germans wanted freedom to function. If they could have their schools without governmental interference, fine! They were willing to build them and pay for their progress. German immigrant nuns, especially School Sisters of Notre Dame, Ursulines and various branches of the Sisters of the Precious Blood, made heroic sacrifices in the interests of Catholic education.

The Irish-American parishes were also blessed with the presence of many immigrant sister-teachers, and a generation later with the zeal of many young women who wanted to be teachers, some in religious congregations, some in other schools. But this was some years ahead. The more immediate problem was the arrival of so many poor people in the eastern cities whose Protestant populations by mid-century were no longer willing to show the broadmindedness of the Lowell town fathers. By that time many members of other Christian denominations so identified America with Protestant Christianity that they took the attitude, albeit unconsciously, that Catholics had rights not from their human nature or the Constitution of the United States, but as Protestant concessions.

Certain up-state New York communities, led by Poughkeepsie, proved an exception. At St. Peter's Parish in 1873, the parishioners worked out a system similar to that tried in Lowell 40 years before. The parish leased its classroom space to the school district during normal school hours. The Board of Education hired the teachers, with the approval of the Catholic parents, and covered other expenses. Complaints were minor, some directed at the religious garb of some of the nun-teachers, others about religious symbols or pictures on the walls. Other communities in New York, Corning, Lima, Westbridge, Waterlivet and Ogdensburg quietly followed suit.

But most Catholic parishes had to provide their own schools without state aid while supporting public schools. By 1884, when the bishops at the Third Plenary Council urged the establishment of a school in every parish, four out of ten Catholic parishes had parochial schools. Some priests and bishops, mainly of Irish ancestry, opposed this recommendation on various grounds. Archbishop John Ireland of St. Paul felt that while the expense was already too great, the Church was reaching only one-fourth of its children. The New York social reformer, Father Edward McGlynn, had gone to public schools himself. He saw less danger there for Catholic students than along the alternate path of withdrawing from the mainstream of American life. Father David Phelan, the controversial editor of the highly successful and influential newspaper *The Western Watchman* in St. Louis, felt that too many parochial schools were foreign enclaves on the American landscape. The German parochial pattern, Phelan and others felt, did not introduce the children of immigrants into American life. It prepared them, instead, to live as German-Catholics in a rural enclave on the St. Croix River in Minnesota, the Republican River in Kansas, or the Kaskaskia River in Illinois.

The supporters of Catholic parish schools did more than defend the Germans. They were ready to reject even the Poughkeepsie Plan as unsatisfactory for Catholics. Influential Bishop

Bernard McQuaid of Rochester, New York, for instance, disapproved of it in 1889.

Archbishop John Ireland of St. Paul, leader of those prelates who looked on American ways as ideal, and wanted Catholics in the mainstream, spoke out clearly and soon. In a speech at the meeting in St. Paul of the National Education Association the following year (1890), Ireland recommended the Poughkeepsie Plan as a means of educating children in a Catholic atmosphere, adjacent to the public school framework, which still provided quality religious instruction and gave them the benefits of tax-supported education.

Many promoters of this plan felt that some of their opponents, more often pastors and bishops than lay people, were concerned more with control of "their" schools than with the total good of the Catholic community. If difficulties arose in one Catholic area in the Midwest where the school boards, made up entirely of Catholic laymen, cooperated with local church officials, almost always any problem that arose came from the side of the churchmen. Archbishop Ireland's speech called forth support and opposition. One of his strongest supporters, Father Thomas Bouquillon, Belgian-born Professor of Theology at the Catholic University of America, went beyond traditional American Catholic views and gave to the state unusual power in the area of education. His pamphlet evoked response from college professors and higher ecclesiastics. Among Irish- American bishops, Bernard McQuaid of Rochester and Michael A. Corrigan of New York joined with Frederick F.X. Katzer of Milwaukee and other German-Americans of the midwest in opposing Ireland's proposals. At times the controversy seemed an Irish-German brawl, at other times a fight between professors at the Catholic University of America and those at universities under the auspices of religious orders.

The St. Paul prelate tried the plan in two Minnesota towns, Faribault and Stillwater. Had he started quietly, and, above all, had it been possible to find a group of Protestant parents, equally anxious for religious education for their children, to sponsor schools in their towns at the same time, the plan might have endured. Unfortunately, no Protestant group wanted to take the onus of supporting Catholics in such a controversial matter. Lutheran communities, generally prosperous and frequently rural, were willing to defray the cost of separate schools. The two trial Catholic-public schools in Minnesota soon went back to the old form, and became privately-supported parish schools.

15

Americanizers
Versus Conservatives

When Peter Richard Kenrick succeeded Joseph Rosati as bishop of St. Louis in 1843, he inherited from his predecessor a vast area. Originally a French settlement under Spanish rulers, St. Louis had welcomed Irish and Anglo-Americans. Many of Bishop Rosati's fellow Vincentians were of Italian birth, as he was. The Jesuits who ran St. Louis University had come from Belgium.

Bishop Rosati had welcomed German Catholics to the rich farm lands in Missouri and neighboring Illinois. Scattered throughout his vast territory were many Indians, such as the Potawatomi who had first learned the faith from Father Marquette in the 1670s, and the Osage among whom diocesan priests and Jesuits had been working for several decades. It was truly a "salad bowl" of varied people.

Responding to the realities of the situation, Bishop Kenrick sent priests who spoke German to the German communities, and French-speaking priests to the French villages. As first archbishop in the Central Mississippi Valley, he allowed "national chapels" within English-speaking parishes to strengthen the religious life of the immigrants. He saw these as transitional places of worship on the way to full Americanization that could well come in the second generation. Little wonder then that he came to be called "the father of the immigrant."

Later in the century, after the Civil War, Bishop John Ireland took a different stance. Irish-born, as was Kenrick, and with many nationalities in his St. Paul diocese, the St. Paul prelate wanted instantaneous Americanization. While he worked well with French-Canadian priests, he clashed with many German Catholic clergy and with members of the Slavonic rite.

The nearest confrontation of supporters of these two views came on December 1, 1891 at the golden jubilee celebration in St. Louis of Kenrick's consecration as bishop. In a stirring address, Father Francis Goller, intellectual leader of the German-American priests of the archdiocese of St. Louis, praised Kenrick for his treatment of the immigrant. Goller admitted that the immigrant might have regard for the land of his birth but had greater love for the country that allowed him to stand up in freedom and be a man.

Kenrick saw in Catholic immigration, Goller stated, not a danger but a priceless addition. The Archbishop welcomed all children of the church, in spite of their disparity in language and manner. He based his hopes for a bright future on the unity of the faith. America was a nation, but not yet a nationality, a distinct people. A century later the ideal American amalgam would represent the best qualities of many European nations.[1]

Goller's remarks upset some of his hearers. These men called on Archbishop Ireland for a retort. The St. Paul archbishop wisely saw that a controversial discussion would mar the jubilee dinner. He simply made an innocuous patriotic statement.

As important as the language question was, it still constituted only one of the many controversies of the time. In the last quarter of the century Catholics debated the place of the public schools, membership in the Knights of Labor, the theories of economist Henry George, the setting up of a national Catholic university, the best ways to promote temperance, the participation of Catholics in secret societies and in interfaith gatherings, and the alleged heresy of "Americanism."

All these issues reflected the central question, the adjustment of Catholics to the American environment. With Archbishop Ireland were Bishop John J. Keane, President of the Catholic University of America, and Msgr. Denis J. O'Connell of the American College in Rome. The veteran Archbishop Kenrick symbolized many issues of the conservatives, but Archbishop Michael A. Corrigan of New York and Bishop Bernard J. McQuaid took the active leadership of the group. Most of the German-American clergy, principally working in the ecclesiastical provinces of Milwaukee, St. Louis and Cincinnati, camped in conservative environs.

The Americanizers held that Catholicism and the institutions of the United States were admirably suited to each other. The prospects of the Church were brighter in the open society of the United States than in the tradition-bound states of Europe. They called for flexibility and adjustment. They criticized the tendency to view American civilization as too materialistic or basically incompatible with the beliefs or inherited values of Catholics. They opposed the use of foreign languages and the continuance of cultural traditions not in accord with American practice. They wanted speedy assimilation.

The conservatives pointed to the indisputable Protestantism and the periodic nativism of Americans. They stressed, in opposition, a preservation of Old World traditions that bulwarked the faith of the immigrant. They supported parochial schools and strictly Catholic organizations. The German-American Catholics tied Catholicism with language and culture. They believed that the maintenance of the cultural heritage supported the immigrant's faith. They saw assimilation as inevitable, of course, but they believed it was a slow and natural process—far too slow for Archbishop Ireland.

While the general discussion between the Americanizers and the conservatives had American prelates of Irish background leading both sides (Ireland-Keane vs. McQuaid-Corrigan), in the specific nationality question the German-Americans played a leading role. The issue became essentially a quarrel between Germans and Irish. For one thing, German Catholics resented being lectured on "Americanism" by those who were as much immigrants as themselves.

In his excellent book, *The Conservative Reformers*, Professor Philip Gleason pinpoints these questions:

> Were the Irish-Catholics really closer to true Americanism, as they seem to think, simply because they spoke English? Did the Germans have to drop their language to become real Americans? If they did, would their faith survive? Would their culture survive? Did Americanization require the disappearance of the German-Catholics as a group?[2]

"In their resistance to the Germans," another Church historian of the period, Gerald Fogarty, wrote, "the Americanizers often magnified and sometimes falsified their (the German-Americans') proposals as if they were measures in a conspiracy to preserve German colonies in America."[3] "Some, like O'Connell, even passed themselves off as native-born Americans,"[4] while they questioned the disposition of native-born Americans of German ancestry, such as Bishop Joseph G. Dwenger, C.P.P.S., of Fort Wayne, Indiana.[5]

In 1886 Father Peter M. Abbelen, vicar-general of the Milwaukee archdiocese, carried a petition to Rome requesting a clarification of the status of German national parishes and discussing in general the relationship of Irish Catholics and German Catholics in the United States. Abbelen had his archbishop's approval and had notified Cardinal Gibbons of his mission. Nonetheless many bishops of Irish-American background reacted unfavorably to this petition. They saw it as a criticism of their way of handling domestic problems, and as an effort to gain special privileges for one national group.

Rome granted three of Abbelen's requests but deferred an answer on the last six: there might be parishes for different nationalities within a given territory; in general, children should remain in their parents' parish until they grow up; and rectors of national parishes might gain the status of "irremovable pastors" in accordance with the Third Plenary Council.[6] The involved Roman procedures led to a mistranslation of the second answer. As a result of this error, Bishop Richard Gilmour of Cleveland unjustly reprimanded Father Faerber of St. Louis. Gilmour had to retract his remarks in this instance; but he retaliated with a severe attack on Abbelen and the *Pastoral Blatt*,[7] a monthly theological journal for priests.

The entire Abbelen affair stirred up rather than calmed the Irish-German controversy. The Americanizers spoke more sharply; the German-Americans, in turn, became even more sensitive to the status of their parishes and to other infringements of their "rights."

Sixty-five German-speaking priests from various dioceses gathered in Chicago for the first meeting of the newly-forming German-American Priests' Society in February, 1887. Under the chairmanship of Vicar-General Henry Muehlsiepen of St. Louis, the conferees planned a huge meeting of German-Americans to be held the following September in Chicago, along the lines of the public demonstrations of faith, called *Katholikentage*, then common in the German states.[8]

The first German-American Catholic General Assembly met in Chicago on September 9, 1887. Leo XIII sent his blessing; and on the following day, the first assembly of the German-American Priests' Society opened. The priests elected Henry Muehlsiepen president, and William Faerber first secretary, both members to the St. Louis archdiocese. The conferees expressed devotion to the Pope, the parochial school system, and the Catholic press, and furthered the immigrant home in New York to bear the name of the Holy Father, Leo House.

The German-Americans were barely holding their lines against the attacks of the Americanizers when in 1891 a severe blow shattered their position. Seven countries, including Canada, had sent representatives to a Lucerne (Switzerland) meeting of a group of societies for the help of immigrants that bore the name of the Archangel Raphael. Unfortunately, no representative of the United States attended the session. In a statement called the *Lucerne Memorial*, the delegates made eight major recommendations for dealing with Catholic immigrants to the United States. The memorial asked for separate churches and schools for each nationality, and priests who spoke the respective languages; and thought it desirable to have representatives of each national group in the episcopacy. They asked the Holy See to sponsor mission seminaries to train priests for work among immigrants in the United States, as Bishop Giovanni Scalabrini of Piacenza was doing for Italian immigrants; and to encourage the formation of St. Raphael societies in all Catholic countries of Europe whence the immigrants came.

In itself the document seemed harmless; but reports of it that came to the United States proved disastrous for the German-Americans. A series of cablegrams attributed the memorial to the German nationals alone, omitting the other six nationalities that took part. These cables misquoted the moving spirit behind the memorial, the zealous German layman, Peter Paul Cahensly, and accused him of having consulted Hurd von Schloezer, the Prussian minister to the Holy See, on the document. The wording of these cables, incidentally, developed in the minds of "the Americanist Agent to the Vatican," Monsignor Denis O'Connell, and Monsignor Eugene Boeglin, a Vatican correspondent.[9] Finally the reports accused Cahensly of asking the Pope to appoint bishops of various national ancestry because "the Irish bishops in the United States only nominate Irish priests, who do not know the languages spoken by the immigrants."[10] Cahensly's membership in the Prussian parliament brought the wholly-unjustified allegation of political inspiration and pan- Germanism. Actually, along with other members of the Central Party, Cahensly opposed Bismarck.

Charges piled on countercharges. In June 1891, unfortunately Cahensly made an imprudent remark in an Associated Press interview. He said: "It is a well-known fact that the Irish in America try to obtain all the bishoprics possible for themselves."[11] The reaction was bitter, even though the actual picture seemed to validate Cahensly's charge. Except for Milwaukee, midwestern cities with heavily German Catholic populations regularly had Irish bishops. A native of County Cork, John Baptist Purcell had served as bishop and archbishop of Cincinnati from 1833 to 1883. Dubuque had Irish-born bishops for half a century and then received an American-born prelate of Irish ancestry, before its first American of German ancestry. Even though St. Louis had more German priests and people than Irish priests and people, Peter Richard Kenrick and John J. Glennon, both born in Ireland, and John Kain of Irish ancestry, would govern the church for over a century. To succeed Kain the bishops of the Province listed three men of Irish ancestry; the priests of the archdiocese named only two, with a third candidate of German-Swiss birth. When made aware of this fact, a future Archbishop of St. Louis, John J. Glennon expressed astonishment at the inclusion of a non-Irish name.

If few Germans reached the hierarchy, even fewer Poles got there. The only native of Poland to reach the fullness of the priesthood was a monk of the Order of St. Basil the Greater, Soter Stephen, chosen first Ukranian bishop of the United States in 1907. The Italo-Americans would have already become the most numerous group of Catholics in America late in the 20th century before an Italo-American became an archbishop.

Sometimes the Americanists deliberately misrepresented their opponents. They projected this basically domestic Church struggle into the wider arena of American life to win public and political support for their viewpoint. They failed to see strength or catholicity in diversity. Eventually they drove a quarter of a million Ruthenian Catholics into schism, because they would not acknowledge the ancient privileges and customs of those devoted people, especially their tradition of a married clergy.

The Catholic leaders of the St. Raphael Society in Europe, on their part, did not view the United States as a nation with its own characteristic ethos. Amid the intense nationalisms of contemporary Europe, they simply thought of it, as Father Goller did, as a place where Germans, Irish, Bohemians, Poles, and others currently resided. Ultimately, it would become a "nation." And Rome took a similar official view in this matter: it still treated the United States as a mission country.

The American Catholics of German ancestry found themselves in the jaws of a vice. Their dedication to the cause of a German-American Catholicism seemed to be dangerous and divisive both to the Catholic Church and to the American national community. The backlash of the Lucerne Memorial identified them with the Prussian regime that had expelled many of them. They went on the defensive psychologically, and moved into the last years of the 19th century embittered by the controversy, profoundly disheartened and with dwindling self-confidence.[12]

In 1897 the entire matter of Americanism leaped the Atlantic and took a strange turn. A colleague of Isaac Hecker, Father Walter Elliot, had published a biography of his mentor in 1891. It had little impact in the States. But six years later a young French priest, Felix Klein, added a special introduction to the French edition. He contrasted Hecker's opening to the modern world, his intelligence, independence and individuality, with the ties of the French clergy to the stodgy ways of the Bourbons. More readers perused the preface than the book.

Abbe Charles Maignen, who identified Catholic hopes with a restoration of the Old Regime, attacked Klein's preface in several issues of a scholarly journal. Gradually he attacked the entire book and Hecker personally. Royalists and conservatives drew up a list of theological errors they attributed to Hecker and called the body of beliefs "Americanism."

Instead of condemning Maignen and his associates for the serious sin of scandal, Rome took their words seriously and did a great injustice to the American people. It lumped a number of beliefs and practices—some reflecting American views, some unknown to Americans, and some rejected by them—called the mess "Americanism," and condemned it.

16

Catholics and Justice to the Worker (1880-1891)

While late 19th century workers in the Catholic cities of the Rhineland, Northern Italy or France claimed to be Marxist, their brothers and sisters who had come to America kept the faith. It was another magnificent triumph of American Catholicism. In recent years, scholars have probed the many factors that helped workers keep the faith.

The would-be industrial worker, coming into Paris from the rural areas of France met an already committed cadre of socialist workers on the assembly line. If any workers were still practicing Catholics, as they may have been in a pre-factory day in the city or in the rural villages of their origin, they had no leadership, either among churchmen or fellow workers.

The immigrants coming from Slovenia or Slovakia to the mines of Pennsylvania or Illinois or the upper Iron Range of Minnesota met few Marxist workers in the pits. Most early miners were Irish Catholics, or "Cornish Jacks," as the first immigrants from Cornwall in southwestern England were called, men usually of Congregationalist background. The hours of work may have been long, the wages low, accidents common, conditions scarcely better than serfdom in the old country, but hope of better days lay ahead.

Further, these Slavic immigrants had not come alone. Others from their area had come at the same time, including, quite often, a priest of their own nationality. They might have ser-

75

vices in the basement of the German or English-speaking church until such a time as they could build their own place of worship. When that time came, the building became more than a chapel for Holy Mass. The adjacent parish hall became the second center of their lives after the home. Here they recreated, met friends, heard their native language, talked of old times across the sea, shared news of the villages whence they came, welcomed newcomers every spring, forgot the hard work of the week in the mines or industrial plants and looked to a brighter future, if not for themselves at least for their children.

The American Catholic community gave to these workers their first widely recognized labor leader, Terence Powderly. Described as "a man of nimble wit and fluent tongue," he had been the Mayor of Scranton, Pennsylvania, before being chosen the Grand Master Workman of the Noble Order of the Knights of Labor, America's first great labor union in 1878. An idealistic man, Powderly looked beyond the immediate interests of the working class to urge a wide-ranging reform of the entire economic system, the "public-be-damned" capitalism of the "Robber Barons" of banking and industry.

Powderly spoke of a "destiny of Labor" to lead the nation to a new plateau of justice but not by engaging in politics or strikes. Instead he urged the formation of marketing and manufacturing cooperative enterprises long before the individual states had laws to safeguard the development of cooperatives. He sought to lessen the workday from ten to eight hours and to insure greater safety and healthier conditions on the job. He frowned on industrial warfare and favored arbitration. He wanted all workers, skilled and unskilled, native and foreign, black and white, craft and industrial, in one big union. His plans reached too widely.

Ritual marked the fraternal organizations in the 1880s, and most rituals in the western world tended to resemble one another. The Knights of Columbus, for instance, followed a ritual similar to that of the Knights of Pythias. The Knights of Labor followed other societies. Further they had to adopt rules of secrecy in order to protect their members from blacklisting by employers.

An employer would fire any man who joined a union and sent the names of the union men to other firms so that these honest workers would be driven out of town or into destitution. The newly-formed state police usually protected "property,"—really the interests of the industrialists against the basic welfare of the worker. City governments often pitted poor men who were policemen against their fellow poor who worked in industrial plants. Industrialists hired secret police and private detectives belonging to the Pinkerton Agency to spy on workers. Further they cared little for the safety or health of the men on the assembly line. Some large employers owned the houses the worker-families lived in and the stores where they purchased food and supplies. There were, of course, still many family-owned enterprises in such home cities as Milwaukee for instance, where the owner lived on the hill a few blocks from the plant, knew all the workers by name, and had concern for the welfare of employees and their families. But most major employers were going in a different direction.

Besides the "black-list," large employers often resorted to the "yellow dog contract," another device later declared illegal by the Congress of the United States. In this arrangement a prospective employee had to agree never to join a union if he wished to be hired. No wonder American workers sometimes reacted with violence, especially during coal, steel and railroad strikes.

A group of Irish coal miners in Pennsylvania, who gained the nickname "Molly Maguires," occasionally brought on the "accidental" death of a hated shop steward or manager. These unfortunate mine officials happened to fall down a mine shaft or into the path of a switching engine in the yards. Spies for the Pinkerton Agency associated the legitimate laboring people with the murders perpetrated by the "Molly Maguires." Further historians have had difficulty in finding out how many of these so-called "murders" really existed, and how many had their origin in the news releases of the Pinkertons. The agency had certainly failed Union General George B. McClellan during the Civil War with its consistent overestimating of the size of Lee's Confederate forces, thereby abetting the hesitancy of the over-cautious but competent young general. They gave a mythical

"Missouri Kid," by the name of Rudolph, the glamor and gun-slinging skill of the James boys or the Dalton gang who had terrorized parts of the state a few years earlier. Local research-ers are still trying to make sure that the "Missouri Kid" really existed as the Pinkertons described him.

A great crisis arose for the organized workers of America and the Catholic Church in the late 1880s. In 1886 many of the Knights in Chicago became involved in May Day strikes. Half of these strikes failed. In the midst of labor disorders, the Chicago police set out to disperse a protest meeting of workers in Haymarket Square on May 4. An unidentified individual threw a bomb. Seven policemen fell. Their companions opened fire. In all, several dozen people were killed or injured. The courts blamed five foreign-born anarchists who had advocated violence and condemned them to be hung.

During 1885 railroad workers went on strike against Jay Gould, a powerful financier with the social consciousness of a rogue elephant. In lowering wages while profits were high, Gould evoked such ill-feeling that the governors of Missouri and Kansas intervened to preserve the rights of the workers. After a quiet year, the rogue elephant broke loose again in 1887 with another lowering of wages. In response to his arbi-trary action, 9,000 shopmen struck for a recognition of their union. They set out to stop all rail traffic in a five-state area by removing essential mechanisms from the locomotives.

When Grand Master Workman Terence Powderly pledged the support of the Knights of Labor, only one priest spoke out and wrote in defense of the workers. He was Father Corne-lius O'Leary, pastor of the town of DeSoto, Missouri, 30 miles south of St. Louis where the Missouri Pacific Railroad had its shops. An Irish immigrant, with a strong chin, a challenging gaze and the physique of a track-layer, he had won a state-wide reputation as a vigorous writer in a regional "religious controversy" several years before. He prevailed upon Richard Graham Frost, a former Congressman, and son of a locally prominent Confederate General, to defend indicted workers. O'Leary himself testified in behalf of the railroadmen before the Curtin Committee of the House of Representatives. Though he sometimes seemed excessive in flaying the railroad bosses, a careful perusal of the congressional report of his testimony leads the objective observer to the conclusion that O'Leary acquitted himself well, at times brilliantly, and performed a significant service to the public and the cause of justice.[1]

As the strike wore on, the people along the right-of-way gradually lost their sympathy for the workers. They needed the food and the supplies the railroad ordinarily brought; but the trains were not moving. The workers, not the owners, had stopped the engines. The general public wanted the walkout to end.

Even though Powderly opposed the use of force, violence broke out. There were no instant-replay cameras to see who started the trouble. The average citizen blamed the strikers, and eventually those who called the walkout. The strike failed dramatically, and that loss had its part in the ultimate decline of the Knights.

His archbishop removed Father O'Leary from his pastorate, and left him without a base of operations. In contrast, the Grand Master Workman of the Knights of Labor, Terence Powderly, acclaimed him as the only priest who spoke out in defense of organized labor before Pope Leo XIII wrote his encyclical *Rerum Novarum.*[2]

In the meantime, the Canadian Archbishop Elzear Taschereau of Quebec had expressed his worries about the Knights of Labor in a memorandum to Rome back in the late summer of 1883. The answer was long in coming. But when it came, Rome condemned the Knights along the lower St. Lawrence. Bishop James Healy in the neighboring non-industrial diocese of Portland, across the border in Maine, followed the Canadian course. Bishops Charles J. Seghers of Oregon and Francis S. Chatard of Vincennes expressed hostility to unions during a discussion of secret societies. And when one realizes that the Grand Army of the Republic and the Ancient Order of Hibernians were among those "secret societies" considered for condemnation, one might well wonder how the Knights could escape. Fortunately Archbishops James Gibbons of Baltimore and Patrick Feehan of Chicago threw their weight in support of the workers' organization.

Among the Archbishops, opposition came from an unexpected source. The dean of the American hierarchy, Archbishop Peter R. Kenrick of St. Louis, had long insisted that local issues be settled locally. He had opposed Roman centralization and papal infallibility, seeing no compelling argument in scripture or tradition. At the same time Kenrick strongly supported the absolute separation of church and state— though he never expressed it just that way. He had studied theology at Maynooth, a school in Ireland that, at the insistence of the British government, required of its students an oath not to engage in politics. He had interpreted that pledge in the strictest way. During the Civil War he refused to let Father DeSmet accept an official chaplaincy lest that fact be used as a recruiting device by the federal authorities. He made no wartime statements one way or the other. He shepherded a divided diocese. Members of his flock fought on both sides: General Rene Paul, and Colonel Julius Garesche with the Union forces; Captain Henry Guibor and General Daniel Frost with the South.

Kenrick had abhorred the violence connected with the railroad strikes a few years previously. He had not approved Father O'Leary's testimony in favor of the railroad workers before the Curtin Committee of the House of Representatives. Since his successor destroyed most of Kenrick's personal papers, no indication appears in any extant material to explain further why this latter opinion overweighed his general anticentralization feeling. For once in his long and otherwise surprisingly consistent career, Kenrick deviated from his usual policy. He went out of his way to confer with the Archbishop of Quebec on the matter. He prevailed upon Archbishop John Baptist Salpointe of Santa Fe to join him in opposition, thus dividing the American archbishops. The most decentralist of men forced the matter to 2 to 10, thus breaking unanimity of approach. The matter would go to the center—Rome. Fortunately the Archbishop of Baltimore was convinced that a Roman decision against the Knights of Labor would have disastrous effects on the entire American Church as well as on the American Catholic workers.

To add a dramatic element that might have seemed contrived in the average piece of fiction, Rome named Archbishops James Gibbons of Baltimore and Elzear Taschereau of Quebec cardinals at the same time in 1887. On the day he first spoke in his titular church in Rome, Santa Maria in Trastevere, the new American cardinal gave a remarkable address. He hoped to open the encapsulated Roman minds that struggled so valiantly—and often in vain—for freedom for the Church to function in their native Italy, in Bismarck's Germany, in anti-clerically governed France and Spain and Portugal, and yet continually denigrated the freedom of America.

"I proclaim with a deep sense of pride and gratitude," Cardinal Gibbons exclaimed, ". . . that I belong to a country where the civil government holds over us the aegis of its protection without interfering in the legitimate exercise of our sublime mission as ministers of the Gospel of Jesus Christ.

"Our country has liberty without license, authority without despotism . . .

"Her harbors are open to welcome the honest immigrant . . .

"Yes, our nation is strong, and her strength lies, under Providence, in the majesty and supremacy of the law, in the loyalty of her citizens to that law, and in the affection of our people for their free institutions . . ."[3]

Unfortunately Rome never came to understand the value of American institutions for many years, still looking on our church-state relations as a temporary concession. But Rome did heed Cardinal Gibbons' insistence that labor as well as management had rights; and that the interests of the half a million Catholics belonging to the Knights deserved as much attention as the concerns of the few employers. Rome hesitated to condemn the Knights.

This action of Rome had repercussions far beyond the range of the Knights of Labor. Actually that union was soon to give way to a less idealistic and expansive form of organization, the American Federation of Labor. But the leaders of the American

Church had stood with the American workers in the face of great public hostility in their first attempt to organize a nation-wide union.

Rome went a step further on an international scale. In 1891, just four years later, the Holy Father Pope Leo XIII, who had named James Gibbons Cardinal of the Church, issued a letter to the whole church on the Condition of Labor. This "encyclical," as such documents were called, took its name from the first words of the Latin text *Rerum Novarum* (colloquially "revolution"). It was to prove the *Magna Carta* of the labor movement and brought enduring fame to Pope Leo XIII. Calling the lot of many laborers "little less than slavery itself," he upheld the right of the workers to unite in labor organizations, condemned class warfare and urged cooperation between capital and labor. The conservative press coupled him with socialists and anarchists as a rabble-rouser. That was the price even a pope paid in asking for justice to the oppressed in those days of "conspicuous consumption."

17

Individual Catholics in Social Reform (1890-1914)

Since the vast majority of immigrant Catholics were working-class people who had to fight long battles for social justice, many individuals, lay people and priests, besides Terence Powderly, Cornelius O'Leary and James Cardinal Gibbons, spoke out against unjust conditions over the years. Since the Irish had been accustomed to struggle for survival in their homeland, one need express no surprise that many of these reformers were of Irish background. What is surprising is this: even with so many of their fellow Gaels crowded in eastern cities, several rural leaders were Irish-Americans.

One of the most colorful and influential among social reformers of the late 19th century, Mary Elizabeth Clyens was the daughter of a refugee from Ulster. Her father, one of the few Catholic farmowners in Northern Ireland, had to flee his homeland for protesting the way the British authorities ineffectively handled the boatloads of grain from America during the famine. He brought his wife and children to upstate New York. The well-educated Mrs. Clyens taught Mary Elizabeth Latin and French at home and instilled in her a love of literature.

During the Civil War, two Clyens brothers were killed and their father dragged off to the deathcamp at Andersonville, Georgia. Mary Elizabeth taught school to support her mother and younger brothers and sisters. Wages were so poor at the upstate New York public schools that Father John

Schoenmakers could offer her a larger salary at the Osage Mission school in Kansas. She went west.

At the age of 19 she married a 30-year-old pharmacist, James Lease. They attempted to homestead in west-central Kansas, only to lose out to drought, grasshoppers and low prices for their crops. She joined the newly-organizing People's Party and soon became the leading Populist orator.

The Populists urged government ownership of railroads, telephones and telegraph lines—or at least stringent regulation of them; a graduated federal income tax; the popular election of senators; a law setting an eight-hour workday; the introduction of the initiative and referendum; and the free coinage of silver. The farmers of the nation generally failed to advert to the changes due to the increase in production brought on by farm machinery and the growing competition from overseas producers. They tended to blame all their trouble on the bankers and railroad men.

The party sent Mary Lease throughout the West and South pleading the cause of the farmers and helping many Populists win places in the state and national legislatures. She herself almost became the first woman senator of the United States, even though Kansas had not yet allowed women to vote. But it was not to be. Her legislative influence remained indirect. Over the years she gradually drifted from the Faith.[1]

Another Irish Catholic who moved west and took a front-center place on Populist platforms, Ignatius Donnelly, also gradually drifted from the Church. He had supported other social reform movements before he took part in writing a fiery preamble to the platform of the People's Party. Born in Philadelphia in 1831, he had studied law and moved to Minnesota in 1856. He served in the United States Congress from 1865 to 1869, was Lieutenant Governor of Minnesota from 1869 to 1873, and member of the Minnesota Senate from 1874 to 1878.

Looking on bankers and financiers as public enemies, he attacked them unmercifully in two papers he edited over the years, the *Anti-Monopolist* and the *Representative*. He also wrote a popular utopian novel *Caesar's Column* that gave a preview of the 20th century as he saw it in imagination. Fantastic to his contemporaries, his predictions, such as radio and television, are commonplace to moderns. He portrayed the United States of 1988 as ruled by a ruthless financial oligarchy and peopled by an abject working class.[2] A fluent speaker, Donnelly laced those "public enemies," the financial manipulators, as eloquently from the platform as he had done with the pen. But his remedies did not match the wisdom of his criticism.

In the elections of 1892 the Populists made solid gains in the states of the South and West; and in 1894, an off-year election, they sent ten representatives and five senators to the National Congress. The Populists looked forward to 1896, believing that they, like the Republicans of 1856, were on the threshold of a big victory. The Democrats seemed bereft of leadership and the Republicans offered nothing for the average American. But success evaded them.

In 1896 William Jennings Bryan put new life into the Democratic Party with his Cross of Gold speech. He supported several important goals the Populists sought. Many of that party urged their fellow Populists to go with Bryan but to choose their own vice-presidential candidate. Donnelly strongly disagreed. He wanted the People's Party to keep its own identity. But those who favored Bryan dominated. Time vindicated Donnelly's stand. The Populists never recovered from coalescing with the Democrats in that election. Donnelly died five years later, still supported by many Populists for the vice presidency.

As if in recompense for losing Terence Powderly, who drifted from the Church in his later years,[3] the Church gained an even greater labor leader, John Mitchell of the Mine Workers, who came into national prominence early in the 20th century. He married a Catholic, Catherine O'Rourke, and joined the Church. A compact man of medium height, Mitchell dressed in conservative black and moved with such controlled reserve that immigrant miners in Southern Illinois thought him a priest.[4] Whether or not he looked like a priest, he talked like Leo XIII.

When advocates of unrestricted capitalism spoke of labor as a "commodity," he responded that "the commodity sold is a human creature, whose welfare in the eyes of the law should be of more importance than any mere accumulation of wealth on the part of the community."[5] He defended the labor movement against the socialists who thought it catered to the capitalists and the capitalists who looked on it as a conspiracy in restraint of trade. As Leo XIII had stated, he insisted: "There is no necessary hostility between capital and labor."[6]

When President Theodore Roosevelt discussed with him a proposal to set up a commission of arbitration during the coal strike of 1902, Mitchell asked that a "Roman Catholic prelate" be on it "as the great mass of miners were Roman Catholics."[7] The President did ask Bishop John Lancaster Spalding of Peoria to serve on the Commission.[8]

A contemporary observer of the social scene will wince at the utter disdain the mine owners showed for John Mitchell and even more at their cavalier attitude toward President Theodore Roosevelt. They seemed to look upon the President as a national chief of police who should send troops into the mines to do their bidding—as Lincoln had sent troops south "to end the rebellion."[9]

Mitchell did not get everything he wanted, but at least, with the President's help and the Republican fear of losses in the coming off-year election, the miners won a few points. The vast majority of the parish priests had stood with their miner-parishioners. Eleven years later Mitchell was able to assert that "the Church is today emphatically on the side of union labor."[10] This was a far cry from the days before *Rerum Novarum*.

Another labor leader, the editor and poet, Ralph Chaplin, looked on the Church as a conservative organization hostile to everything he stood for in the public area, and did not come into the Church until late in life. When given a copy of *Rerum Novarum* by a friend a few years before his death, he remarked: "How different my life would have been had somebody shown this to me fifty years earlier."[11]

A famous social reformer, Mary Harris "Mother" Jones, broke the pattern. Born a Catholic, she clung to the Faith throughout her life. The granddaughter of an Irish political martyr, and daughter of an exile, she married a Memphis iron molder. The yellow fever epidemic of 1867 carried off her husband and their

four children. She moved to Chicago and took work as a seam-
stress. The Haymarket riot of 1886 turned her into a labor agi-
tator. She began to participate in demonstrations throughout
the country, especially in the coalfields of West Virginia and
Colorado just before World War I. She taught a revolutionary
gospel straight out of the New Testament. She urged workers
"to pray for the dead and work like hell for the living." When
she died in 1930 at the age of 100, a huge crowd, which included the Secretary of Labor and the President of the AFL,
attended her requiem Mass at St. Gabriel's Church in Washington.[12]

Like Terence Powderly, Ignatius Donnelly and Mary
Elizabeth Lease, several social reformers among the Catholic
clergy found the atmosphere in the Church as stifling as the
national ethos back in the days of conspicuous consumption.
One such was Father Thomas Hagerty, who was already a convinced Marxist before he was ordained in Chicago at the age of
30. He looked on Marxian socialism as an economic doctrine
compatible with Catholicism. Actually Hagerty's views were
closer to those of Leo XIII than to some of the bishops of the
Southwest where he worked in a parish.

He gained wide notoriety by calling for an endorsement of
the Socialist Party by the Western Federation of Miners at their
Denver convention in 1902. Instead of returning to his parish in
Las Vegas, New Mexico, Hagerty toured the mining camps with
Eugene Debs, the Socialist leader. Archbishop Placide Chapelle
of Santa Fe took away Hagerty's pastorate and disclaimed any
responsibility for him. The free-wheeling cleric then edited the
Voice of Labor, the official organ of the American Labor Union.
He took a significant part in the launching of the Industrial
Workers of the World (IWW), a militantly socialist organization
in 1905. He helped to frame the Industrial Union Manifesto, an
invitation to all workers to revolt against both craft unionism
and capitalism. Shortly after, for reasons never disclosed,
Hagerty left the socialist movement. He taught Spanish in Chicago and worked as an oculist. Eventually he drifted into skid
row "a free and happy soul," in the words of one of his few old
associates who ever ran into him.[13]

Another social reforming priest of great talent who left the Church was John R. Slattery, first Superior-General of the Josephite Fathers. He too felt the failure of his fellow Catholics to respond to the demands of social justice, in this instance in the cause of the blacks. He also delved into Modernism as Father Hagerty had studied Marxism.

Father Slattery's father had made a fortune in the contracting business in New York in the years shortly after the Civil War. In spite of his wealth, Slattery had to endure continual ridicule as one of the few Catholics at City College of New York. While at Columbia Law School he decided to give up his wealth and become a missionary. He looked upon the treatment of blacks in America as parallel to the Irish experience and he decided to devote his life to that apostolate. He became the first Superior General of the Josephite Fathers, a society working in the black apostolate. In seeking justice for the blacks, he found that his fellow Irish Catholics were the blacks' chief obstacle in seeking admission to the trade unions. He looked upon the seeming indifference of the vast majority of Catholics as even more frustrating to the cause of evangelization of the blacks.[14]

When Modernist theories made their appearance on the American horizon, the highly reflective Slattery became acquainted with the main views of the movement. He translated some of the writings of French modernists and gradually drifted from the Church. In 1906, he wrote an article "How My Priesthood Dropped from Me,"[15] and sometime later, an even more significant article "The Workings of Modernism."[16]

Two other social reforming priests of the late years of the last century ran into trouble with their archbishops but did not leave the Church. The previous chapter has discussed the work of Father Cornelius O'Leary who ran into trouble with one archbishop for his public support of labor. He lost his parish, wandered around during the years of another archbishop, but finally won a new parish from a third.[17]

Another priest stayed loyal to the Faith even though churchmen excommunicated him. When handsome, popular and brilliant Father Edward McGlynn was ordained in Rome in 1860, many predicted that he would soon occupy a prominent place in the American Church. Instead he took antiestablishment views on church-state questions, and his concern for the poor won him over to programs of social reform that did not sit well with several archbishops of New York.

He supported the theories of Henry George, a social-reforming writer who advocated a theory of taxation that had great appeal in Ireland but little for rich and conservative Americans, Catholics as well as Protestants. Archbishop Corrigan may not have been rich, but he was conservative. When Father McGlynn spoke in behalf of Henry George's candidacy for the position of mayor of New York, the Archbishop imposed silence. Father McGlynn rebelled. He insisted that he was simply exercising his right to speak as an American citizen. Corrigan threatened severe penalties and Rome summoned McGlynn to explain his position. McGlynn refused to go abroad.

George lost his bid for the mayor's chair. McGlynn lost his parish, but appealed. After some years, Roman authorities lifted the excommunication. But the great work Father McGlynn might have done remained undone. After his death parishioners erected a statue in his honor. Interestingly, no New Yorkers erected a memorial to the Archbishop.[18]

Up to this point Irish surnames have dominated this discussion of social reformers. But in the view of at least one Catholic historian of Irish-American background, the German-American enclave produced one layman of unusual competence and wide social concern.[19] Early in the 20th century Frederick Kenkel became editor of *Amerika*, the leading German Catholic daily in the country. He had a scholar's mind and learning and brought his intellectual energies to focus on the social and moral issues of the moment. His wide-ranging editorials caught attention in many parts of the country.

Leaders of the *Central Verein*, an enduring German-Catholic organization centered in St. Louis, sought his advice. Recently reorganized, the society was looking for a new focal point for its activities. Following Kenkel's advice, the *Verein* adopted social reform as its primary activity and goal. Kenkel became director of its newly-established central bureau and editor of the *Social Justice Review*. That journal pioneered among Catholic magazines in making social reform its principal concern. This work made him "the most influential German Catholic layman in the country."[20]

While Kenkel clearly identified himself as a conservative and drew inspiration from the Middle Ages, he looked to fundamental changes in the social order through decentralization of economic and political power and communal solidarity. He opposed individualism, secularism, the contemporary climate of capitalism, and political centralization. He promoted many worthy causes such as cooperatives, credit unions, and the liturgical movement.

His greatest work lay in analyzing and criticizing social trends. He believed that Father John A. Ryan's recommendations for social legislation and his fellow *Central Vereiner* Peter Dietz's simple trade union approach to social reform were stopgap measures. In spite of their different approaches, Father Ryan still praised the *Social Justice Review* for avoiding "the edifying and empty platitudes that so often passed for social analysis."[21] The work of that distinguished professor at the Catholic University of America will come up in a later chapter.[22]

18

Catholic Colleges Continue

In the early decades of this century most of the Catholic colleges and universities, situated in metropolitan areas, inconspicuously but determinedly taught the sons and daughters of immigrants and prepared them for Christian marriage or for careers in many fields. The parents of these students and the lay teachers and members of religious congregations who staffed these schools made great sacrifices in the interests of religious education.

Unlike the urban schools, in that it stood at the outskirts of a smaller city rather than in a large metropolitan area, the University of Notre Dame gained great prestige in the 1920s with an outstanding football program under the leadership of Coach Knute Rockne. This consistent policy of aiming for excellence on the athletic field made Notre Dame the symbol of Catholic manhood in the eyes of other Americans and brought the loyalty of countless Catholics throughout the nation. Men of New York who had never crossed the Hudson lived or died every week of the fall with the fortunes of the "Fighting Irish." These New Yorkers gained the honored name "Subway Alumni." Even out West in the city of Denver, the Notre Dame Alumni Association took part in a wide variety of civic ventures—even when sponsored by the local Jesuit institution, Regis College.

The Newman Center at the University of Illinois led the way in a different direction. Under the progressive leadership of

Monsignor John O'Brien and later Monsignor Edward Duncan, the Newman Center in Champaign developed programs of cooperation in advance of other universities. At first, Monsignor O'Brien seemed to offer the Newman Center as the alternative to the Catholic college. This stance faced a solid wall of Catholic educators. State laws and constitutions differed so widely that a type of cooperation possible in an enlightened commonwealth like Illinois was impossible in other states, such as its western neighbor Missouri, much less in states where the Ku Klux Klan had gained control in the 1920s.

The attitude towards Catholicism at many secular institutions of higher learning until the post-World War II period was at best neutral or condescending, at worst derogatory or insulting. On the campus of an Ivy League school as late as the 1930s a prominent history scholar ridiculed the Catholic Church in America as "an institution run by the sons of Irish washerwomen."[1]

All the while several prominent professors of history, such as Carlton J.H. Hayes, Parker T. Moon and Henry S. Lucas, were finding that a study of history called in question the traditional underpinnings of the Protestant denominations, and so wrote in their widely used textbooks. But while they themselves became Catholics, most historians, whose ancestors may have been believing Protestants, gradually became secularists. The historians looked on Catholics as a benighted people or as the remnant of a once-significant group that sent out great missionaries like Serra and Kino who built lovely missions in the Southwest several centuries ago. Some professors viewed the Church as an "interesting expression of the ethos of ethnics from the South and East of Europe." All the while the climate in most state colleges in rural areas, especially in the west and south, remained positively Protestant. At one of them, as late as the 1970s, ordained Calvinist ministers constituted the bulk of the history department.[2]

The university of a midwestern state founded by French Catholics hired no Catholics on its faculty until the late 1930s when it signed a coach from a southern Protestant College. He turned out to be a Catholic. The university of a southern state founded by Spanish colonists hired its first Catholic instructor shortly after World War II. When the trustees found he was a Catholic, they met to decide what to do. Wisely, they decided to do nothing.

Years later many midwestern state colleges began to enlarge their programs of religious studies. One found a way of getting around Missouri's strict separationist regulations to allow 15 hours of religion in the normal 128 hours needed for a bachelor's degree. The Newman Club and the Protestant Center had to provide classroom space and qualified teachers. The students received credit through religious colleges elsewhere in the state. These were transferred to the university's records with a minimum of red tape. But that's moving ahead of the chronological scheme.

In the years after World War I, Catholic colleges sprang up all over the country. Many of these stemmed from the work of religious congregations. Some mother superiors wanted to have normal schools for their own future sister teachers, and set up schools exclusively for religious. Most, however, were for lay students, principally girls. In general, the Catholic universities were male institutions. Catholic dioceses, religious orders and congregations were to begin and, with the help of dedicated lay people, conduct 309 colleges by the year 1965.[3] These were not facades with no faculty or institutional strength, but enterprises that, for the most part, met high standards of regional accrediting agencies.

Unfortunately, the administrative arrangements of dioceses and religious congregations held back the type of cooperation that might have prevented excessive duplication within an area or even with a religious order itself. At one time, for instance, three Catholic colleges in Buffalo were building libraries.

In Missouri, Catholic educators Father V.F. Corcoran, C.M., of Kenrick Seminary and Webster College and Dean Alphonse Schwitalla, S.J. of St. Louis University's School of Medicine set out in 1924 to coordinate the efforts of all Catholic institutions of higher learning in the area. A group of colleges such as Fontbonne, Webster, and Maryville, and two "junior" colleges worked with St. Louis University on many aspects of collegiate life. All graduates received their diplomas from St. Louis University. Unfortunately, Kenrick Seminary with its noted faculty and alumni did not join in the consortium. Likewise unfortunately, the administrators of the schools did not follow through and seek a common campus area to avoid proliferation of libraries, chapels and other facilities. It would have been highly feasible at the time, but the required statesmanship was lacking.

Successive heads of the Jesuit Educational Association, such as Father Edward Rooney, not a father-rector or a college president, but a representative of the Father General with only suasive powers, had tried to bring about coordination of the efforts of the Jesuits and their 28 colleges and universities. One such was the Macelwane Report of 1933 that among other recommendations urged each Jesuit college to choose an area of excellence and emphasize that. Under that plan Georgetown wisely might have concentrated special effort on international relations, Marquette or Detroit on Engineering, and Loyola of Chicago on midwestern French colonial history. The latter school took several fine steps in that direction, but few other schools followed the recommendation to choose an area of concentration. Several years later a professor at a midwestern Jesuit college drew up a challenging plan for a Great Lakes Jesuit university that would have coordinated efforts of Marquette of Milwaukee, Loyola of Chicago, the University of Detroit, John Carroll of Cleveland, and Canisius College of Buffalo. The Jesuit presidents at these schools failed to respond to the challenge.

St. Louis University, however, did continue to reach for a significant place in the Catholic higher education picture. It built strong departments of history, English and physics during the 30s and numbered several prestigious faculty members, such as James Macelwane in seismology, and Dr. Edward Doisy in chemistry. Father Joseph Husslein, S.J., Dean of the School of Social Work, edited a group of books called the Science and Culture Series; and in conjunction with Bruce Publishing Co., developed a wide Catholic clientele. The Catholic Hospital Association located its headquarters adjacent to the St. Louis University Medical School.

Shortly after World War II, St. Louis University took under its umbrella Parks Air College, a prestigious flight and mechanics school, that had trained more than one out of every ten fliers in the Air Corps during the recent war. With that addition, the University moved dramatically into the field of aeronautical technology.

Members of the University's History Department gained permission to microfilm documents in the Vatican Library. The Knights of Columbus financed this project. In view of the need of proper locale for these microfilms and relying on the great prestige of Pope Pius XII throughout the world at that time, St. Louis University launched a national campaign to build a memorial library to Pius XII. Nationally-known individuals gave their names to the drive.

Georgetown, the pioneer Catholic university in the East, as St. Louis was in the Middle West, had won recognition in the field of foreign service during the years between wars. Its long tradition and location in the nation's capital gave it a continuing prestige. In the 1970s and 1980s John Thompson, one of the first black coaches, developed a spectacular basketball program.

Catholic University of America in Washington had a national base in its location in the national capital, in its name and in the support of the bishops of the country. It developed several outstanding departments and boasted of several distinguished professors, but lacked a widespread lay student body. Further, its religious alumni still did not rival graduates of the North American College in Rome in prestige and power within the Church. In short, until the Catholic University became the alma mater of the average bishop and most of the cardinals in the United States, it would not have the prestige that its founders sought for it.

In the 1970s, Boston College suddenly surged as a national Catholic university due to a number of circumstances not always easy to assess. It was as if all of a sudden Catholic high school youngsters all over the country suddenly thought of going to Boston College. Perhaps it was the atmosphere of New England and the Ivy. Perhaps it was the magic name of Doug Flutie, a spectacular football player who, in spite of his small size, brought fame to the school on the gridiron. But whatever, suddenly Boston College had emerged as a Catholic university center.

During the long term of Father Theodore Hesburgh, C.S.C., Notre Dame assumed such significance that a sociologist at a western state university nominated it as the "Catholic university of the nation." Few set out to challenge his arguments. Notre Dame had the resources, the outstanding faculty personnel, a widespread loyalty among Catholic people throughout the nation, a dedicated and distinguished alumni, and continued publicity stemming from its impressive athletic program.

As educational costs continued to soar after the mid-20th century, many Catholic colleges lessened their Catholic stance to obtain government funds for their institutions or their students. In 1966 the President of the Jesuit Educational Association, Father Paul C. Reinert, Rector-president of St. Louis University, put as top goal for Jesuit colleges the establishment of "the autonomous status of universities, with concomitant obligation to resist directives from ecclesiastical authorities."[4] Both the Jesuit Superior-General Father Pedro Arrupe and the illustrious scripture scholar Augustine Cardinal Bea, had reservations about this "new order."[5]

Catholic university leaders, with Father Hesburgh at the helm, met at Land O'Lakes, Wisconsin the following year, July 20-23, 1967, and insisted "that institutional autonomy and academic freedom are essential conditions for life and growth and indeed survival for Catholic universities, as for all universities."[6] The following year a meeting of the International Federation of Catholic Universities in Kinshasa, the Congo, September 10-17, 1968 agreed among other items that "a juridical tie with Rome is not an essential note of a Catholic institution."[7]

The members of religious orders who ran these schools decided to face the long overdue need of introducing lay persons into their governing boards. Too often these members of the laity were not alumni nor alumnae, much less individuals representative of the many professors who had committed their lives to the institution. And yet the presidents had insisted on seeking freedom from their own religious superiors on "the right of the lay faculty to have a voice in establishing policy."[8]

Some theorists came up with a formula that seemed to suggest that the school really did not belong to the religious congregation but to the general public. Some religious communities even ended up bereft of the building they lived in. A few social observers muted their criticism that this constituted an alienation of church property—to give the plan a chance. But they certainly held that belief.

These decisions disturbed a great deal more people than the Jesuits Father Arrupe and Cardinal Bea. The university presidents did not match their clear-cut statements of independence with an equally-convincing explanation of how the institution would keep its Catholic character. How far did the freedom of a professor go if he or she fought the basic ideals of the institution? What made these distinguished presidents presume that the trustees, faculty, administrators and staff would necessarily remain loyal to the spirit and traditions of the institution? After all, the great secular universities of the country had originally been Protestant foundations that went from clerical to lay control to neutrality even in matters of the beliefs of the founding group.

Notre Dame University flourished in such a vital atmosphere of Catholicity that it could not conceivably move from its traditions. But this total immersion in a Catholic atmosphere was hardly shared by all schools. A prestigious English professor at one of the Jesuit universities whose president had taken a most vital part in the Kinshasa deliberations complained that "there is no way another Catholic much less a Jesuit could get into my department."[9] The man, the last Catholic in the department, died shortly afterward.

In the 15-year period between 1965 and 1980 ninety colleges lost their Catholic identity. Few social observers looked at these moves as a disaster, so prestigious were the individuals who brought them about. But such a loss could hardly go unnoticed. Fortunately, however, most Catholic colleges and universities kept their original commitments by a number of judicious steps.

A few came out stronger and even more dedicated to the Catholic tradition than before.

Some Catholic educators who had temporarily waxed secularistically and promised to ape Harvard—if only they had similar endowments—now kept silent before their colleagues who had always felt their own institutions had values that even Harvard lacked.

In spite of all these changes and tribulations stemming from them, Catholic colleges and universities faced the 90s with renewed confidence.

19

The High and Low
of Catholic Grade Schools

The tremendous growth of the Catholic school system in America amazed the rest of the Catholic world while it dismayed many American advocates of exclusively state-controlled education. By 1900, 3,811 schools enrolled 854,323 pupils. Ten years later 1,237,251 girls and boys attended 4,845 schools.

Citizens of the Pacific Northwest, most of them practicing Protestants, decided to do something about this development. The legislature of the state of Oregon considered a law that required all students to attend public schools. The state had enough anti-Catholic sentiment without outside help. Nonetheless, members of the Ku Klux Klan who had never previously bounced their shrill voices off the Cascade Mountains joined in the shouting. Not even the Kaiser's Germany had tried such tactics for 50 years. Communist Russia alone set an example for these self-acclaimed "preservers of American liberties." The law flowed through a referendum without hitting a snag or "sawyer" in 1922 and Governor William Pierce signed it.

This piece of legislation set out to close all private schools, the Country Days and Andovers, as well as the Christian Brothers High and the Holy Name Academies. Oregon had no place for a Boston Latin School or a Bronx Academy of Science. Educators of the nation should have risen up in indignation at first. None did. The Catholic people of Oregon with the help of the National Catholic Welfare Conference—still alive in spite of misgivings of Roman authorities who looked askance at national episcopal conferences—won a stay from the lower court. When the state of Oregon appealed to the Supreme Court, interdenominational help came to the Catholics from the Protestant Episcopal Church, the Seventh Day Adventists and the American Jewish Committee. Roger Baldwin of the American Civil Liberties Union offered legal assistance, educator John Dewey criticized the law and Oregon, and Nicholas Murray Butler, President of Columbia University, said the Oregon legislature would have disturbed the graves of several founding fathers.[1]

In the meantime, the neighboring state of Washington had begun to push for a similar law. Even after the Federal District Court declared the Oregon law unconstitutional, over 131,000 citizens of Washington voted for the questionable legislation. With little outside help, the few Catholics of Oregon had to defray the expenses of carrying the case to the Supreme Court against Governor William Pierce.

With the unanimous backing of the entire body, Justice James C. McReynolds delivered the opinion of the Supreme Court on June 21, 1925. "The fundamental theory of liberty upon which all governments in this Union repose," he stated, "excludes any power of the state to standardize its children by forcing them to accept instruction from public teachers only. The child is not the mere creature of the state. Those who nurture him and direct his destiny have the right coupled with the high duty to recognize and prepare him for additional obligations."[2]

Since the Catholics of Oregon had won, few gave much thought to the fact that the Court had rendered its decision not on the basis of freedom of religion (the First Amendment) but on property rights (the Fourteenth). By compelling attendance of all children at public schools, the Oregon School Law had deprived the Sisters of the use of their property, a building erected for school purposes.

Catholics had won a great victory for all schools under private auspices. But time showed they had, in reality, won only reluctant sufferance. Many otherwise generous Americans thought they were doing Catholics a favor in allowing them to operate their own schools at their own expense.

Catholic elementary schools continued on their quiet way, giving an extra focus to parish life. Where a parochial school existed, the parish moved with vigor. A parish without a school generally limped along. The Confraternity of Christian Doctrine set out to provide catechetical teachers for students in public schools. The success of the program varied from place to place.

Some Catholics, such as educational theorist Mary Perkins Ryan, pointed out the disproportionate amount of money and person-power American Catholics devoted to the relatively small percentage of Catholic youngsters in parochial schools. One item the proponents of this position failed to assess carefully was the fact that the money came in precisely for the school.

Be that as it may, Catholics owed a tremendous debt to the numerous teaching sisters whose sacrifices made their school system possible. In one archdiocese, in fact, where publicists praised the venerable archbishop for developing fine high schools, the nuns taught in those schools without pay. Their congregations sacrificed for the good of the Church. The "vacations" of these teaching sisters consisted generally in a full schedule of summer university classes at an urban locale as they sought academic degrees.

Only later did various congregations of sisters begin to work together to prepare their members properly for their teaching careers. One such program under the direction of Sister Bertrande Meyers, D.C., began at Marillac College near the Daughters of Charity Motherhouse in suburban St. Louis. Various congregations joined to marshall an outstanding faculty. One religious congregation, previously located only in northern Louisiana, set up its formation center adjacent to the Marillac campus so its young sisters could share the Bertrande vision. Unfortunately, the plan came into being a little too late for it to reach its full potential.

All the while the Oregon School decision had not set well with those who supported absolute separation of Church and State. As early as 1944 Supreme Court Justice Felix Frankfurter began to prophesy that the Court would come "to rue the implications" of the Oregon School Case.

When various citizens challenged a New Jersey arrangement that provided bus fares for parochial school children in 1947, Frankfurter opened fire behind the scenes in the conference room. While liberal Justice Hugo Black thought the provision permissible and led the support group in the case of *Everson vs. Board of Education*, Justice Frankfurter badgered, harassed and pushed his opponent into a secularly absolutist premise for his majority opinion: "Neither a state nor the federal government . . . can pass laws which aid one religion, aid all religions, or prefer one religion over another."[3]

This paved the way for an ultimate antireligious stance by courts and legislatures. When men began to talk of federal aid to education several years later, the Barden Bill proposed to make funds available only to those states that allowed no money at all to students in religious institutions. If Louisiana made textbooks available to pupils in parochial schools, it could receive no money. If New Jersey provided parochial students with transportation to school, as the Supreme Court had so recently approved, New Jersey pupils could not share in their government's grants. Presidents Jefferson and Madison would have expected this type of legislation from their contemporary, Frederick the Great of Prussia, not from fellow Americans who claimed them as progenitors of their "liberalism." Yet these modern "liberals" supported this unwarranted exercise of federal power.

All the while an interesting development was taking place in many German Catholic communities of the Middle west on the elementary and high school levels. Citizens of these rural areas began to look with interest at the "Faribault" plan originally devised in some ways against their ancestors. They liked what they saw. As a result, the ones who had always built their own parochial schools, and whose ancestors had looked with disfavor on Archbishop Ireland's proposals, adopted similar arrangements. They had built their schools. Now they leased them to the school district between nine and three o'clock five days a week. Nuns taught religion during the pre-rental 8-9 hour in the morning. Since the nuns had gained teaching certification, the local board would hire them as full-time teachers.

In these German Midwestern communities, the county school buses brought the children from their farm homes to school. The library would more likely contain the life of Elizabeth Seton than that of Mary Baker Eddy, and that of Peter Jan De Smet than of Elijah Lovejoy, that of John Carroll rather than of Cotton Mather. But they were "public" schools.

In one Protestant-Catholic community in Kansas, the public school board took the initiative in uniting two pre-existing high schools, one public, one Catholic, into one town high school. The Catholic children remained in the previous Catholic school building, now rented by the School Board during the hours nine to three. The "public" children continued in the district-built building. The public children could go to the Catholic building for Latin and mathematics—courses not available in the other building, and Catholic children took manual training and "home ec" in the public building. The two sections shared publications, dramatics, and sports programs. Unfortunately, too few Midwestern towns shared the excellent arrangements, sometimes because of outside interference through court decisions, sometimes through local misunderstanding on one side or the other; perhaps even more because the local people in that town did not advertise their excellent plan and asked writers to say nothing of it, lest outside "busy-bodies"—to quote the Protestant mayor of the town—might disrupt it.

In the late 1950's several Catholics in St. Louis began the first unit of what gained the name of "Citizens for Educational Freedom." Rev. Virgil Blum, S.J., a Jesuit professor of Political Science at Marquette University, drew up the rationale behind this movement in such books as *Freedom of Choice in Education*.[4] One could summarize Father Blum's basic premise in this way: The Constitution does not require a citizen to give up one right to enjoy another. If an individual enjoys freedom of religion, for instance, that person does not have to give up freedom of speech to exercise that right. One cannot be compelled to forego freedom of the press in order to vote. So if parents wish to exercise their freedom of choice in education guaranteed by the Constitution, and reaffirmed by the Oregon school case of 1925, then they should be allowed freedom to choose schools for their children. Yet, if they so choose, they must forego all benefits provided by the state for education. They have to give up one right (state help toward the education of their children) to enjoy the privilege of choosing the accredited school they wish for their children. It would be as if one who wished to enjoy a glass of beer at a reasonable price would have to purchase it from a state-owned brewery and not from Busch or Coors or Millers. Or as if one who wanted to enjoy freedom of the press would have to write in Shakespearean English and not in modern English, much less in Yiddish or German or Polish or Italian.

After reading Father Blum's books, a group of St. Louisans met at the home of Martin Duggan, the city editor of the *Globe-Democrat*, the morning newspaper. Among the participants was Judge Anthony Daly of neighboring Madison county in Illinois. He had often written on the rights of children in private schools to receive state aid in mastering "the nonreligious ingredients of education." Out of this meeting grew the first unit of the Citizens for Educational Freedom.

The members invited a black lawyer to help in the drawing up of their constitution so that no one might claim it was a segregationist group. Quite interestingly, the black community did not further participate in the program. The "Black Caucus" in Congress followed secularistic patterns even though most black people remained deeply religious.

The Citizens for Educational Freedom grew and solidified. Dr. Dan McGarry, Professor of Medieval History at St. Louis University, wrote on the views and progress of the Citizens for Educational Freedom in a number of excellent magazine articles. Units began in other Midwestern states and had great success in Minnesota, among others. At the outset many coastal Catholics looked upon the program as a typical Midwestern simplistic approach. Each generation of coastal Catholics had to learn that initiatives for change usually came from the broad prairies between the Alleghenies and the Rockies.

With the departure of a great number of nun-teachers from the Catholic school system in the late 1960s and the decline in vocations, many parochial schools found difficulty in getting teachers. The number of parochial schools dropped from 10,879 in 1965 to 8,149 in 1980 and the enrollment of 5 million went down to 3.2 million.[5] But to the surprise of all but a few sociologists who studied the real trends and tendencies, interest in Catholic education grew stronger.

As the number of nuns and religious men available for teaching declined sharply, more lay teachers moved into the classrooms and the administrative offices. The pay might be less than in public education but the basic attitudes of the system made teaching a more pleasant experience. Gradually, it became clearer that the Catholic populace, no longer predominantly poor immigrants but now mostly prosperous middle-class citizens, wanted a religious education for their children such as they themselves had enjoyed.

In the meantime, the American public school, once Protestant-oriented in fact though not in the mind of the law, had become so secularized, and in many places actually anti-religious, that many Protestants, especially Baptists, began to open their own schools. Lutherans had long supported their own parochial schools. Mainline Protestants of wealth had always sent their children to private schools that abounded near big cities. In one large Midwestern city no prominent citizens sent their children to public schools. In the early 1980s a private school in suburban St. Louis numbered among its alumni three senators: two from Missouri and one from California. One social observer remarked: "The public school is no longer the 'established church' of American Protestants."

In the meantime, the courts of the nation had given to public schools responsibilities no educational system could be expected to handle: to lead communities in bringing about better race relations. At first, the courts simply outlawed segregation in the schools. Then they urged forced busing to integrate schools. Ultimately, courts urged busing of students to create "racial balance" in all schools. Some of these court demands piled injustice on injustice in the name of securing justice. Little wonder disruption replaced education in some places.

All the while parochial schools continued their educational traditions, and innovated in two areas. Even though Catholics formed a minority in many former slave areas, they pioneered in integration in such states as Missouri, Arkansas, Alabama and North Carolina. In many cities of the nation they opened their inner-city schools to black Protestant children whose parents wanted a more traditional education.

Catholic educators woke up one morning to find that they were winning acclaim as institutions that kept the fundamental values of order, discipline and regular progress. Strangely, this change stemmed not from a theological viewpoint but from the educational philosophy of the Catholic schools that had rejected the false premises of the French philosopher, Jean Jacques Rousseau, whose unstable views that questioned authority and the natural origin of the state underpinned so many public school systems.

The Citizens for Educational Freedom began to urge a system of "Vouchers" whereby the state funds for education would go to the school of the parents' choice. The fight for justice in the schools had ceased to be a Catholic versus Protestant struggle, but a confrontation of parents who believed in religious education and an assortment of secularists.

In spite of the political power of the National Educational Association that admitted no weakness in the philosophy or current policy of the urban public school, signs of change stood strong on the horizon.

20

Catholic Social Reform After World War I: Industry and Politics

Two significant social reformers of the post World War I period grew up in the rural areas of southern Minnesota. One, Father John A. Ryan, went east to be a professor at the Catholic University in Washington, and concentrated on the industrial problems in our cities. He ended up as a key figure in the social action programs of the National Catholic Welfare Conference. The other, Father Edwin Vincent O'Hara, did likewise, but along a different path. He went west to be a pastor in Eugene, Oregon and an advocate of farm reforms. His career will come up in the next chapter.

Even though Pope Leo XIII had come out strongly for social reform in his Encyclical Letter of 1891, *Rerum Novarum*, most Catholic social reformers, priests and lay people seemed to be moving out on their own initiative. The officialdom of the Church in America took no strong stands as a unit, even in support of the encyclical of Pope Leo. In one way the fault lay with Rome itself. Up to that time, the Curia had discouraged united action on the part of the American bishops. Collegiality ranked low on the list of Roman policies.

In this impasse a group of bishops led by Bishop Peter Muldoon of Rockford, Illinois, followed the urging of Pope Benedict

XV's representative, Archbishop Bonaventura Cerretti, at the Golden Episcopal Jubilee celebration of Cardinal Gibbons in February 1919. The visiting delegate took a new tack and recommended to the American hierarchy unity of action in regard to social and educational problems.

Bishop Muldoon called on Father Ryan at Catholic University to draw up a program of social reconstruction. Father Ryan had earned his licentiate in moral theology, *maxima cum laude*, from the Catholic University in Washington in 1902. He had published articles on labor organization in the *Catholic Encyclopedia* and had written extensively on the "living wage." He had analyzed the respective ethical obligations of management, labor and stockholders in modern industrial society at a time when all three thought the clergy should stay in the sacristy. He obviously was the best man to draw up this program.

The bishop's program called for legal protection of labor organizations, minimum wage legislation, participation of the workers in management and ownership, public housing, health and old age insurance, restrictions on women and child labor, control of excessive profits and income through regulation of rates and progressive taxes on inheritance and income, effective control of monopolies, the establishment of cooperative stores, and the continuation of the War Labor Board that had been set up to promote better relations between management and workers during the war.

In that same year, 1919, Father Ryan became Dean of the School of Theology at the Catholic University, published *Church and Socialism*, coedited a collection of social documents entitled *The Church and Labor*, and became director of the Social Action Department of the National Catholic Welfare Council (later Conference).

Father Ryan paddled against the current along the Potomac during the 20s. The Supreme Court rendered null some of the social reforms of Woodrow Wilson's first term, such as the Clayton Anti-Trust Act. Firms encouraged company unions instead of independent locals of the American Federation of Labor. President Warren Gamaliel Harding spoke of "Normalcy." That meant, in effect, that business could do what it pleased. In 1924 the Republicans chose the colorless and close-lipped Vice President Calvin Coolidge instead of the progressive reformer Senator Robert Lafollete of Wisconsin. A committee of the New York State Senate, investigating seditious activities in 1929, pointed a menacing finger at "the socialist tendencies of a group of Catholics under the leadership of the Rev. Dr. Ryan."[1] Social reform would have to wait for the impetus of the Great Depression in the fall of that same year, 1929.

That catastrophe gave a platform to an eloquent pastor of Royal Oak, Michigan, Father Charles Coughlin. Using the pulpit techniques of the better revivalist preachers, the Michigan priest soon was speaking to an entire nation every Sunday evening. Countless Americans heard the voice of a priest for the first time in their lives. Coughlin mastered the catch-phrase. He first challenged the American people "to drive the money changers from the temple of our nation." Later he offered the alternative of "Roosevelt or Ruin." Gradually he moved more closely to the political arena. At first he made people aware that, while all knew the name of the president, many did not know the name of their own congressmen. He urged them to be more attentive to congressional elections. By 1936, however, he had become disillusioned with President Roosevelt, denounced the chief executive and publicly supported a third-party candidate, Representative William Lemke of North Dakota. Nominee Lemke received even fewer votes that Governor Alfred Landon of Kansas, the Republican nominee.

During those years Father Ryan moved in a different direction. He had supported the former Secretary of War, Newton Baker, not Governor Franklin Delano Roosevelt for the presidency in 1932. But he found that FDR favored many of the reforms he had long advocated and became a strong supporter of the President. Father Ryan called the Wagner Act of 1935 the greatest piece of labor legislation the Congress had ever enacted.

Father Ryan began to counter Father Coughlin's radio addresses with strong talks over the air waves. Conservative Catholics criticized him. He received over a thousand abusive letters. One seaboard Catholic weekly suggested that both "political priests" could profit by a lengthy period of total silence in a contemplative monastery.

During FDR's second term Father Coughlin allied himself with various one-issue advocates, took a strong midwestern isolationist position as war broke out in Europe, and denounced the "hidden power of high finance" that he associated with individuals of one particular nationality. His *Social Justice* newspaper, once a positive enterprise, gradually became a lurid sheet. He seemed to look on Hitler's Germany as the one bulwark of the then militarily-weak West against the threat of the mighty Red Army.

It was a time of excessive communist propaganda in the United States. The "Commies" used all the techniques in their arsenal, such as innuendo, and "guilt by association." These techniques, later used by U.S. Senator Joseph McCarthy, came to be called "McCarthyism." In actuality, the Committee on Un-American Activities of the U.S. Congress, chaired by Representative Martin Dies of Texas, had identified these devices as communist while young Joe McCarthy was still in college in Wisconsin.

In 1937 a new archbishop came to Detroit, Very Rev. Edward Mooney. He suggested strongly that the growing Shrine of the Little Flower, Father Coughlin's Parish Church in Royal Oak, Michigan, needed the pastor's undivided attention. To the edification of countless people, the priest who had held a center-stage position for so long exercised his many talents within the more restricted sphere of his parish for almost a quarter of a century. By that time most of those people had grown old who remembered the positive influence of his early years during Hoover's administration when he was the only clergyman in the country who pointed out the need of public concern for the social welfare of all the people. A new generation remembered only his negative years.

Father Ryan refrained from public support of President Roosevelt in the election of 1940, adhering to the nonpartisan position of the National Catholic Welfare Conference. But he had rejoiced at the Fair Labor Standards Act of 1938 that brought many improvements for the work force, including minimum wages and maximum hour levels, and restrictions on the hiring of children. He felt this act culminated his lifework. He had so strongly supported the social legislation of the late 30s that when he became a domestic prelate many referred to him as the "Rt. Rev. New Dealer." His final glory came with the publication of "The Church and Social Order," a statement of the American bishops that endorsed almost every reform John Augustine Ryan had supported for three decades.

In the meantime many other priests had been active in industrial reform: professors like Father (later Bishop) Francis Haas, Father Raymond McGowan and William Kerby at the Catholic University of America, and writers like John Cronin, S.S., and Joseph Husslein, S.J. The Association of Catholic Trade Unionists (ACTU) grew strong in many Eastern cities. Priest educators, among them John Friedl of Kansas City and Philip Carey of New York, soon began "labor schools"—evening sessions for members of unions where they learned parliamentary procedure, public speaking, and other practical devices for leadership in the unions.

Fathers John P. Boland of Buffalo and Leo Brown of St. Louis were among those who began to serve as representatives of the public on national or state labor boards. The nation had many Catholic labor leaders over the years. Philip Murray, Chief of the CIO and later George Meaney, head of a reunited AFL-CIO, and still later César Chavez of the Farm Workers were merely the top of the list of the many Catholics in the movement.

A great number of Catholics in the national Congress had their part in the enactment of excellent social legislation. A U.S. Senator from a western state, not a Catholic himself, publicly attributed the nation's great social legislation to Catholic and Jewish members of Congress from the states of the North and the East. He recited a long list of names to support his assertion. Even a cursory perusal of the *Congressional Record* bears this out. Two Catholic Secretaries of Labor, Maurice Tobin and James Mitchell, helped the cause of the worker.

As a result of these efforts, the vast majority of Catholic workers in the industrial cities continued to live vital Catholic lives.

21

Catholic Social Reformers: Rural, Racial and Pacifist

Even though an overwhelming number of American Catholics lived in the industrial cities of the north and east, many Catholic farmers, mainly of German-American ancestry, lived in the country. Three midwestern counties, Clinton in Illinois, 40 miles east of St. Louis, Stearns in Minnesota in the diocese of St. Cloud, and Ellis in western Kansas, stood out for their many strong Catholic parishes.

In 1929 Father Edwin V. O'Hara, the previously-mentioned pastor in Eugene, Oregon, who had been studying the problems of Catholic farming families, became director of the new Rural Life Bureau of the National Catholic Welfare Conference. A year later he completed a religious survey of his own county and published a report on his findings. He set down what he thought the church ought to do in "A Program of Rural Catholic Action." In 1923 he called together Catholic rural leaders for a meeting in St. Louis. Eighty persons—bishops, priests, brothers, lay men and lay women—heeded the call and set up the National Catholic Rural Life Conference with Father O'Hara as Executive Secretary. His "Program of Rural Catholic Action" became its canon.

Father O'Hara served as Executive Secretary until he became bishop in Great Falls, Montana, in 1930. After 19 years of leadership in Montana, he became bishop of Kansas City, Missouri, a large and influential city in the "Heartland of America," but not a leading Catholic center. The archdiocese of St. Paul would have been a much better place for Archbishop O'Hara (his title was personal; Kansas City remained a diocese) to exert the great influence that he could have had. Northern bishops promoted the movement well: Bishop Aloysius (later Cardinal) Muench of Fargo, Bishop Peter W. Bartholome of St. Cloud, Minnesota, Bishop Vincent Ryan of Bismark and Bishop William Molloy, a priest of North Dakota who became Bishop of Covington, Kentucky. Father Luigi Ligutti, who had a significant background of rural work at Granger, Iowa, became Executive Director of the National Catholic Rural Life Conference. When Monsignor Ligutti went to Rome to serve as the Holy See's permanent observer for the Food and Agriculture Organization (FAO) of the United Nations in 1948, Father Edward O'Rourke of the diocese of Peoria eventually succeeded him. He later became bishop of his native diocese.

Editor and writer Monsignor Vincent A. Yzermans credits the National Catholic Rural Life Conference with three principal contributions: the Confraternity of Christian Doctrine, the development of the International Catholic Migration Commission, and the development of international awareness in our agricultural heartland.[2]

The Catholic Rural Life Movement had to face strong opposition from outside and unconcern from within the Catholic community. Since the Catholic population of the U.S. was heavily urban, many city-bred bishops seemed to ignore their rural areas. Some even looked upon the country parishes as places to isolate or discipline "problem" priests. The absence of wide distribution of stable Catholic farm families remained a great weakness of the Catholic body.

In a third area of social reform a member of the hierarchy holds a significant place, the area of racial relations. Here the name of Joseph Cardinal Ritter who became Archbishop of St. Louis in October 1946 stands out. Over the years the archbishop regularly denied that he had been sent to St. Louis to integrate the Catholic community. But many indications point to that.

Shortly after his arrival in St. Louis, someone pointed out to him "the black parish church." "I thought we had only Catholic churches," he allegedly remarked. Be that as it may, he soon had an occasion to remedy the situation. St. Joseph's High School for Blacks needed larger quarters. Instead of urging the rental of an old or the building of a new school, he ended the segregated pattern. All Catholic children should attend the grade school in their parish, and the high school in their district. St. Louis University and its prep school, St. Louis University High School, were the only integrated schools in the entire state at that time.

In view of the fact that state law forbade integrated schools, and presuming this limitation also applied to private schools (as the previous archbishop had seemed to believe before St. Louis U. integrated), a group of lay people formed a committee to seek a court decision. The archbishop called to their attention a law of the church that brought automatic excommunication to anyone who called in state authorities against their bishop when he was acting within his capacity as spiritual leader. The group dispersed.

One might well wonder how a heavily industrial state like Missouri, far from the plantation South, entirely surrounded by free states, Illinois to the East, Iowa to the North and Kansas to the West, could have been a slave state and remained a segregated area for so long. But so it was.

Missouri emancipated the slaves in 1865. At that time Archbishop Peter Richard Kenrick set aside a parish for the Blacks on a citywide basis, much as he allowed national parishes, German for the Germans, Bohemians for the Bohemians, Polish for the Polish, Croatian for the Croatians and later Italian for the Italians. The only problem was that while the other nationalities had a priest of their own group, the black parishes always had white priests.

In 1939 when the Provincial of the Society of the Divine Word wanted to send two black priests to St. Louis, Archbishop John J. Glennon, later Cardinal, presumably had ignored his letter.[2] Archbishop Ritter was moving against the traditions of the state and the positions of his predecessors.

Catholic schools such as St. Scholastica's Academy in Fort Smith, Arkansas, Springhill College in Mobile, Alabama, and the Catholic school in Wilmington, N.C., followed St. Louis' example and led the way in the respective states. In 1954 the nation caught up with these pioneering Catholic institutions with the Brown vs. Topeka decision that ended "separate but equal" schools that had been separate but were rarely equal.

Many Catholic lay people, nuns, brothers and priests had worked toward the day of justice. Among nuns, Blessed Katherine Drexel founded the Sisters of the Blessed Sacrament to work among native and black Americans and devoted her fortune of 21 million dollars to the cause of education of these disadvantaged young people. She was the most prominent of the many religious women, black and white, who worked for the improvement of the lot of the oppressed. She founded Xavier University in New Orleans in 1915.

Among early Catholic black lay leaders, Daniel Rudd of Cincinnati had edited and owned the *American Catholic Tribune* late in the last century, the only successful newspaper printed for and by black Catholics at the time. Lincoln G. Valle edited the *St. Louis Advance* in the early years of this century. Dr. Thomas Turner, a college professor who was to receive an honorary degree from the Catholic University of America on his 100th birthday, had set out in 1914 to build a strong federation of black Catholics. He had the support of St. Paul pastor Father Stephen L. Theobald, the first black priest educated entirely in American seminaries. Many white priests involved themselves in the apostolate among blacks, especially members of the Society of St. Joseph and of the Society of the Divine Word, a congregation that took many black candidates for the priesthood and would number five black bishops among its members.

In an entirely different area of social reform the name of one woman stands out above all others. Her fellow Catholic Americans revered Dorothy Day for what she was rather than for what she stood. Her public stance emphasized pacificism even during the war with Hitler and Hirohito. But it was her total unworldliness and dedication to human betterment that made Dorothy Day's name a byword throughout the land.

Along with a born-Catholic, the French "peasant-philosopher" Peter Maurin, convert Day began the Catholic Worker movement in May 1933. In their publication, *The Catholic Worker,* they advocated a cooperative world society based on free association. Social betterment would come from changed individuals who would reject middle-class ways and values and form their own communitarian ventures.

Day and Maurin set up houses of hospitality in cities and Catholic Worker farms in various parts of the country. Maurin wrote his striking thoughts in simplified free-verse that caught the immediate attention of the reader. He spoke also in these cryptic phrases. Unfortunately, after his death in 1949, a new generation grew up that did not know him. Dorothy Day continued her work through the Cold War and gained new importance when the younger people of the country turned to pacificism during the Vietnam War. One could well predict that the name of Dorothy Day will long be remembered in benediction.

Shortly after her death, the Claretian Fathers and Brothers distributed a fitting prayer for private circulation that hailed Dorothy Day as "friend and partner of the poor, guiding spirit of the Catholic worker, . . . early, often lonely, witness in the cause of peace and conscience, eloquent pattern of gospel simplicity . . . disciple of the Lord" and concluded with the hope that we might continue her "gift of self to the needy and her untiring work for peace."[3]

22

Capable Women and Steadfast Men

European clerics regularly raise their eyebrows that American Catholic women ask of their church greater recognition of their talents, skills and expertise. If these clerical gentlemen would open their eyes and ears on the rare occasions they visit this country or meet American women in Europe, they would see a distinct American pattern. Too often the only women they meet are their East European servants, women who are so happy to slip out from behind the Iron Curtain that they are willing to cook and keep house for Roman ecclesiastics.

American womanhood includes a number of poets, college presidents, hospital administrators, legislators, writers, historians, commentators, professors, engineers, canonized saints—as well as housekeepers. One nun stands among other great Americans as representative of her state in the hall of statuary. Mother Joseph, of the Sisters of Providence, represents her adopted state, Washington. She began six hospitals and countless schools during the frontier days in the Pacific Northwest.

American Catholic women have enjoyed educational advantages available to few of their continental counterparts. The vast majority have completed secondary school. Many have finished college. A significant percentage has graduate degrees in a variety of fields, including theology. Almost all of America's 309 Catholic colleges were founded and staffed by women for women students.

America has not yet had a Catholic woman as President—nor any woman for that matter. But the Democratic Party did nominate a woman for vice president in the election of 1984, a member of the House of Representatives from New York, Geraldine Ferraro, a Catholic. Another member of the church, Ella Grasso, had been elected Governor of Connecticut in 1974. The people of various states have elected significant Catholic women legislators. Among them, on the national stage, Clare Booth Luce, editor, playwright, and foreign corespondent, represented Connecticut in the 78th and 79th Congresses (1943-47). Later on she served her country as Ambassador to Italy.

Lenore Kretzer Sullivan of Missouri had a much longer career in the United States House of Representatives (1953-77). Mrs. Sullivan so doggedly fought for the interests of the average American that she won the sobriquet "The Consumer's Advocate." President Harry Truman referred to her as the "best member of the House" during his years in public life. Even those who recognized "Harry's" tendency to tout his fellow Missourians admitted the validity of this statement.

Typical of the Catholic women legislators on the state level, Senator Eudochia Bell Smith advanced much of the best social legislation during her days in the Colorado legislature.

Many more women, Catholic as well as others, have taken part in civic or church work in a wide variety of fields. Several outstanding individuals in these areas deserve our grateful memory both because of their distinguished individual efforts and as typical of many other achievers.

In her chapter "Women in Washington," in the bicentennial book, *Catholics in America*, Professor Dorothy A. Mohler of the Catholic University of America singled out two women who devoted their lives to social action, Agnes Regan and Jane Hoey. "Both were remarkably gifted women," Dr. Mohler wrote, ". . . daughters of Irish immigrants, . . . from families of nine children. . . . Westerners by birth, . . . committed to the service of others. Their commitment was based on a strong Catholic faith."[1]

Agnes Regan of San Francisco represented her archdiocese at the organization meeting of the National Council of Catholic

Women in 1920. Shortly afterward, she became its executive secretary, a position she held for 20 years. In this capacity she worked for better immigration laws, improvement in health care, and restrictions on child labor.

Nebraska-born Jane Hoey held a key executive position on the federal level. In 1936 she became the first director of the Bureau of Public Assistance, Social Security Board. She held this post for 17 years. Her main task was administering relief programs. She was president of the National Conference of Social Work and served as U.S. Delegate to the United Nations Social Commission.

Both Agnes Regan and Jane Hoey received the Siena Medal given annually to an outstanding Catholic woman. Miss Regan won the papal decoration *Pro Ecclesia et Pontifice*. Catholic University gave her name to a residence hall for social work students. Three universities conferred honorary degrees on Miss Hoey and she received two awards from the New York School of Social Work.

The Church has canonized two foreign-born missionary nuns, Philippine Duchesne and Frances Xavier Cabrini, and recognized the holiness of two women born in the United States, St. Elizabeth Seton and Blessed Katherine Drexel. All the while, it has seen fit to raise only one man, St. John Nepomucene Neumann, C.Ss.R., to the ranks of the canonized.

An American missionary bishop told of an experience he had in the early years of his ministry in a Latin American country. The wealthier women of his city who had attended Catholic colleges in the States planned to give him a birthday gift. They asked what he wanted, a new chalice perhaps, or a vestment designed by Belgian nuns. He responded: "The greatest gift you could give to me would be to bring your husbands with you and the children to Mass on Sunday."

The women were surprised, baffled, utterly perplexed, in fact appalled. Had he asked them to make a pilgrimage on foot to the top of Mt. Aconcagua, it might have been conceivable. But to suggest what their husbands might do was in no way within their ken.

They went to Mass on Sunday and brought their children. Their husbands considered themselves "Catholics" but the macho image allowed no place for church attendance; a public expression of religion was foreign to the men of that country, even more so if they held political office.

An American woman does not have to tell her husband to go to church. Further, she has a great background in religion herself. Perhaps she attended a Catholic college, as her Latin American sisters did. But she came from that institution with a far more mature outlook on religious matters and the relation of the sexes than the young ladies from South of the Border.

Obviously, the European Church has not sufficiently challenged the great qualities of American women of both laity and religious institutes. It is even less excusable that the American Church itself has been so slow to recognize the great skills of American Catholic women.

A priest stationed in Rome during the time of one of the many controversies that mark church life made this remark: "The two most frank and intelligent appraisals of the entire matter came from two American women, mother generals of their religious congregations. Men played politics and slanted their answers to accord with the Roman power structure. The American nuns gave their personal judgments frankly, without reference to the opinion of this or that cardinal head of this or that Roman congregation."

The Catholic women of America are not alone in giving a distinct tone to their religious outlook. American Catholic men do, also. When the future Pope Paul VI visited the North American College in Rome on his return from the United States, he expressed his pleasant surprise at the vital Catholicism among men in America. He had not been used to such in his native land nor had he any experience with such manly Catholicism anywhere. Throughout much of the Latin American world, for instance, the macho image prevails; the he-man is the rough-and-tumble, irreligious, profane person. Religion is a female preoccupation there. Few men attend church regularly in many parishes, and these few are often older citizens.

In the average parish in the United States, on the contrary, the church at Sunday Masses numbers as many males as females. The vast majority of "hard hats," the industrial workers, are family-oriented, church-going family men. The Church stayed with the workers in their day of stress. They in turn have stuck with the Church.

In a letter to Notre Dame University on the occasion of its centennial in the early 1940s, His Holiness Pope Pius XII commended the spirit of Notre Dame. He spoke of the "virility" of the Notre Dame alumnus, and praised the school for instilling the notion that fidelity to one's religious practices "was consonant with the best in American manhood."[2] In its tremendous record on the football field, Notre Dame did over many decades give an example for all to see of a ruggedly manly Catholicism. The Notre Dame man became for many the symbol of American Catholic manhood.

Where but in America would one meet a successful football coach like Vince Lombardi coming out of Sunday Mass or kneel alongside an all-star basketball player at a three-day closed retreat, or find a star linebacker at the communion rail two hours after leading his professional football team to an afternoon victory over the Colts?

The charismatic leader of a Florida parish was a legendary linebacker of the Chicago Bears football team. A Catholic parish in St. Louis celebrated its 75th anniversary jointly with a parishioner's 50th birthday. He was an all-star baseball player and the manager of championship Cardinal teams. Five stars on America's one great World Cup soccer team that beat England in 1951 came from the same Catholic parish, Saint Ambrose "on the Hill," in St. Louis.

"Catholic athletes," a prominent midwestern sports writer stated, "don't wear their religion on their sleeves. They don't ask every other player if he 'is saved.' But they keep the commandments, love their wives and children, and go to Mass every Sunday even when the team plays away from home."[3]

One of the most successful baseball managers, a winner of championships in both leagues, attributed his conversion to the Faith to the example of players on his teams who attended Mass regularly during the baseball season.

The Catholic Church numbered two Chief Justices of the Supreme Court among its members, both devout worshippers at their parish churches, one President, a great number of Senators over the years, countless Congresspersons, judges of state and federal courts, and distinguished governors and mayors. Perhaps the greatest of these governors, John Burns of Hawaii, hardly merited attention from the media on the mainland. But he deserves lasting fame. In many ways the father of his state, he showed the statesmanship that brought the territory of Hawaii into the Union as the 50th state. But his claim to eminence dated long before. Immediately after Pearl Harbor, when otherwise liberal leaders, President Franklin Roosevelt and Governor Earl Warren of California, panicked and herded mainland Japanese-Americans into concentration camps in an amazing violation of civil liberties, Burns, an official of the police in Honolulu, insisted that no one under his jurisdiction would go to jail unless on a specific charge as American law demanded.

Richard Daley of Chicago, the most powerful political figure in the American Midwest, attended the same parish church as mayor as he had done when a newly-married man hoping for a career in politics. A few born-Catholics gave up their religion to advance in politics, but these few pale before the countless American political leaders who remained staunch Catholics.

Top military leaders through the years have been Catholics. Further, the proportion of practicing Catholics who won the nation's highest decorations for bravery in military service match or surpass that of other groups in the nation.

23

Ethnic History:
Realities and Limitations

Many historians have recently come to look at ethnic history to understand the development of the church in America. This wise move provoked interesting studies, and deserves consideration. First, ethnic history can have two related meanings in the American "salad bowl" scene. It can include all nationalities with distinct cultural backgrounds, place of origin in the Old World and neighborhood unity in the New World. Use of the term would include the two largest national groups of 19th-century American Catholics, the pre-Civil War Irish and German immigrants, as well as the 20th-century influx of French-Canadians, Latin-Americans, and Southeast Asian Catholics. A more frequently-used meaning limits ethnicity to the people of the "Second Immigration" from the south and east of Europe (Austria-Hungary, Russia, Italy and the Balkans), who came between the Civil War and World War I. This second meaning will frame this present discussion.

These immigrants from the south and east of Europe came principally to the heavily-industrialized cities of the Great Lakes region, such as Chicago, Milwaukee, Detroit, Cleveland, Pittsburgh and Buffalo, the "Foundry of America," in the parlance of many economic geographers. These newcomers started parishes of their own nationality and language, or located in established parishes of that type. The church was more than the place where they worshipped on Sunday. It was their social center. They might spend their entire holyday there with breakfast after Mass, followed by gossip, games, and general socializing.

The big celebrations of the people took place in the parish hall—the wedding parties, communion breakfasts, the anniversary celebrations. They had Altar and St. Vincent de Paul societies, bowling leagues and soccer teams, and men's and women's sodalities. The parish might also have economic significance if it had begun a credit union or an insurance program.

Some ethnic parishes put out magazines or newspapers for their own parishioners or for all members of that nationality. The newspaper *Hlas* (*The Voice*) went from St. John Nepomucene's Parish in St. Louis to Bohemians all over the country, especially in metropolitan Chicago, rural Nebraska and the southern part of Texas.

Some individuals chose to shun the national parish, choosing to live elsewhere in order to win faster identification as Americans among their Anglo-American neighbors. Many living away from the ethnic neighborhood and its old country language and traditions gradually drifted away from the faith also. Some few even joined a mainline Protestant church. This fact made the national pastors even more anxious to keep the flock speaking the foreign tongue in the ethnic enclave.

Shortly after World War I a surge of nativism brought "hyphenated Americans"—as they came to be called—into disrepute. The ethnics faced ridicule and derogatory stereotypes, and heard ugly names cast upon them—all in the name of an American spirit that claimed all were created equal. Then came the Depression. People had other problems to worry about—food, clothing and shelter. World War II followed.

When the Nazi panzers brought destruction, degradation and death to the homelands of their ancestors, the young men of these ethnic neighborhoods answered the call to the colors with great enthusiasm even before Pearl Harbor. Few areas of the country matched the record of the Italian district of St. Louis, "The Hill." With a total population of 6,300, including the many grandparents who came from near Milan, over 1,100 young men volunteered for the Navy and the Marines or were drafted.[1] The 52nd block on Wilson Avenue in that neighborhood of single-family homes, not apartments or tenements, sent 40 men overseas.[2]

When lights went on again around the world after victory in Europe and the Pacific in 1945, countless ethnics discarded their guns and picked up their books under the GI Bill. Soon Slavic and Italian names began to turn up where few had appeared before, on the faculties of state universities, in the legislatures and the courts, and in the offices of banking and industrial giants.

The nation began to hear a slogan: "Black is beautiful." It made many realize too, that Czech is colorful, Romanian romantic, Polish popular, Lebanese lovely, Greek glorious and Italian ideal. Americans began to appreciate the diverse cultures that had contributed to the nation's rich heritage. People no longer spoke of a "melting pot" where all rich metals were melted into one, but of a "salad bowl" of enriching diversity. The nation looked for "community" and found in the old ethnic neighborhood a long-standing sense of community. The cities sought to restore themselves and found that the ethnic enclaves had not deteriorated, but stood as ordered oases in an urban wasteland. Other areas of our urban centers began to "rehab" and restore themselves.

The second generation Americans who might on occasion have muted their ethnic identity now found their children and grandchildren bragging about their ancestral heritage.

While the "ghetto experience" played its part in the development of these various nationalities, three important segments of the Catholic population had their own secure position outside the ethnic enclave. An earlier chapter has shown that the Maryland Catholics had gained status and position in the early days of the Republic. When many of them moved to Kentucky and on to places in Missouri, Illinois, Arkansas and New Mexico, they brought with them the confidence of the old settlers. They and their ancestors had been around. They were part of the American scene.

The French colonials in the middle Mississippi Valley and in Louisiana and the Gulf areas, as mentioned earlier, had already established themselves in economic and civic positions in their communities before Jefferson purchased Louisiana. They generally welcomed their fellow Catholics of various nationalities.

Converts formed the third category of influential Catholic Americans. One could list, among others, such individuals as Elizabeth Seton, wife, mother, nun-founder, educator and saint, the already mentioned Orestes Brownson, Dr. Moses Linton, and the Barber family. Bishops William B. Tyler of Hartford and Sylvester H. Rosecrans of Columbus; Civil War general, William S. Rosecrans, brother of the bishop; Dr. Edward Pruess leading lay theologian of the late 19th century who brought his four sons with him into the Church; and, in more recent times, Clare Booth Luce, author and stateswoman. These men and women added more than luster to the American Catholic scene. They gave to their fellow Catholics a feeling of profound presence in the mainstream of American life.

Stemming directly from these converts, the influential offspring of converts seemed to offer a distinct flavor to American Catholic life. One name comes dramatically to mind, that of Daniel A. Lord, S.J., pamphleteer, youth organizer, writer and director of pageants, a man of extensive talent and wide influence. Another, Dr. Arthur Pruess, followed in his father's footsteps as a leading lay theologian in a day when America had few theologians, clerical or lay. There were many other descendants of converts who left their mark on the Catholic community.

24

American Catholics and Political Liberty

In the age of dictators between the two world wars (1919-1939) the United States and other English-speaking countries offered the one notable area of freedom in the world. This experience of freedom did not come suddenly, but grew over the centuries.

Historians see the seeds of the constitutionalization of free institutions in the *Magna Carta* in 1215. When the barons of England forced King John to respect their rights as "freemen," they made their demands as peers of the king, not as commoners. But they set a precedent. In later centuries Englishmen of various classes, not just the nobles, would appeal to *Magna Carta* as a precedent to insure their rights.

In 1295 King Edward I summoned to Parliament, along with the nobles and higher clergy, two townsmen from every borough and two knights from every shire. While this parliament had no lawmaking power, it had to approve new taxes, a power that it could gradually enlarge over the centuries. It set the stage for future parliamentary influence.

During that same century the Fourth Lateran Council (1215) recommended that "what concerned all had to be approved by all," an encouragement of the notion of wide representation. Outstanding American historians recognized the Rule of St. Dominic, approved by the popes during that same century, "as a constitutional masterpiece, providing for provinces and chapters of the order, and for representative democracy in its central government."[1]

The friars in each priory elected a representative to the general chapter. He acted as their proxy and committed them to a course of action after debate and decision with other elected representatives. Imperial Rome had set up senates, and kings had councils before with some minimal type of representation. But this was the first time all these essential elements of proper representation were present.

The ideas of the Dominican Fathers and of the Council Fathers—ideas shared also by the military knights of that century—influenced other countries in the Middle Ages. France had its Estates General, Spain its Cortes, and Germany its Reichstag. Unfortunately, in times of crisis, the rulers of those continental countries gained control of the purse, so that they could tax their people without the approval of an assembly of the people and gradually became absolute monarchs by the 16th century.

The King of England, however, could not impose new taxes without the consent of Parliament. From this initial position of power, the members of Parliament during the 14th and 15th centuries gradually gained the right to make laws. This came about through several steps. The members drew up a list of grievances to be presented to the King at the time he asked for new taxes. Later they phrased these grievances in the form of laws. Eventually he granted them the power to pass the laws. Parliament even deposed a king on one occasion during those years.

When the Tudors came into power in the late 15th and throughout the 16th century, they ruled absolutely in fact. But having only a slight claim to the throne, they worked through constitutional means. Henry VIII might have decided to do away with his peerless Chancellor Thomas More or John Cardinal Fisher. But Henry brought it about so that Parliament appeared to make that decision.

Later on, during the 17th century, the days of the Stuart Kings who claimed to rule "by divine right," the members of Parliament could reassert their position. In opposition to the first two Stuart Kings, James I and Charles I, members of Parliament frequently referred to *Magna Carta* and quoted the medieval priest-jurist and noted commentator on the Common Law, Father Henry de Bracton: "The King is under no man, but under God and the law."

During the reigns of the last two Stuarts, and of William and Mary, the members of the King's cabinet who were merely his councillors at the outset gradually became the leaders in Parliament. Finally, the real power came to reside in the leader of Parliament, the Prime Minister, rather than in the King. When, in 1714, England chose German Hanoverian princes as kings, men who could not even speak English, the Prime Minister soon wielded authority, with the King merely a symbol.

This was the English-speaking world the Founding Fathers grew up in. They derived their knowledge of government from a living tradition and from their own practical experience in the procedures of that tradition—in their respective colonies before 1776 and in their state governments and the Continental Congress from 1776 to 1787. Much of what they did grew out of the centuries-long English tradition.

Other features of the American system were distinctly native, but put in by men whose answers stemmed from this ancient tradition. Such were the federal system, the division of powers between local and national government, and the Northwest Ordinance that allowed new states to come in later, co-equal with the original 13. America developed the position of the president who combined the powers of the prime minister with some of the respect given to the king.

Our Constitution divided powers between executive, legislative and judicial departments, an arrangement praised in theory by writers such as Montesquieu. America was the first nation to restrict by law the authority of the government in religious matters. It simply said that the sphere of religion lay beyond the province of the government.

Other English-speaking countries, Australia for instance, tried such procedures as the initiative and referendum. We later adopted these devices of democratization. One or two democratic procedures in England and several of the British Commonwealth countries have offered greater freedom of parental choice in education than the American pattern. Unfortunately we have not tried any of these.

During the two centuries that this advance of freedom was taking place, while European countries enjoyed only an occasional taste of constitutional government, few European churchmen ever came to appreciate American liberties. One can understand this only in consideration of two mind-sets. Most European churchmen had little contact with freedom at any time in their lives. They lived in an authoritarian world. Further, what little liberty came to Europe swept in with the spirit of hostility to religion in the violence and terror of the French Revolution. That liberty took its stance on the wavering sands of unsound ideas of individuals and society, many of them stemming from the writings of Jean Jacques Rousseau, already discussed in an earlier chapter of this book.

Our Revolution, or war for independence from England, involved no hatred of religion; it did not pit class against class, or overturn most institutions of society. Some historians point out that the changes Americans sought were consistent with trends and might possibly have come about peacefully had more farsighted statesmen led England at that time. They assert that America might have been the first self-governing Dominion of the British Commonwealth rather than an independent country.

European churchmen understood "freedom" only in the light of the excesses of the French Revolution. They had little contact with American constitutional development or the gradual path to freedom followed in England. They ran the government of the Church according to the only patterns they knew, the absolutist, centralized system that had brought endless sorrow and repeated revolts to Europe.

25

Midwestern Catholicism: Distinctive, Dynamic

Just before the opening of Vatican II, the *Ave Maria* magazine, published by the Holy Cross Fathers at Notre Dame, Indiana, carried an article on the distinctive and dynamic qualities of the Church in the American Midwest.[1] What would probably have been a message of limited significance had a wide sway when Joseph Cardinal Ritter of St. Louis brought it to the attention of his fellow prelates of the midcontinent, such as Albert Cardinal Meyer of Chicago.[2]

Both of these archbishops spoke out strongly on main issues facing the Council Fathers. In the first session Cardinal Ritter was to join with Cardinals Bea, Lienart, Suenens, Alfrink and other north European cardinals in opposing the outmoded statement on Revelation presented to the assembly by a preparatory commission.[3] He would insist on a clarification of the position of bishops, and the status of the Roman Curia, and was to agree with Tubingen theologian Joseph Ratzinger that the function of the papal office was "not monarchical rule, but rather coordination of the plurality that belongs to the Church's essence."[4] Cardinal Meyer would take a decisive part in the declaration of religious liberty, both by serving on the central four-prelate commission, and by arranging a special meeting with Pope Paul to insure the final decision on that important matter.

The progressive attitude of these prelates reflected the greater interior of the country whence they came. The creative triangle bounded by St. Louis, Notre Dame and Collegeville, Minnesota, saw an amazing proportion of American Catholic initiatives. Few significant movements grew up in the South, the Serra International in the Pacific Northwest and only the temperance movement, the Knights of Columbus, and one or two others in the East.

Laymen in Cardinal Ritter's own archdiocese of St. Louis, the oldest in the Middlewest, began the first St. Vincent dePaul Society in the 19th century and the first *Senatus* of the Legion of Mary in the 20th. St. Louis was the first center of the Vincentians, the Religious of the Sacred Heart and the Sisters of St. Joseph of Carondelet, at one time the largest sisterhood in the nation. Many congregations of religious opened their novitiates in the area. The Archdiocese pioneered with a foreign mission in Bolivia.

The German-American fraternal and social action organization, the Central Bureau, chose St. Louis as its national headquarters in the last century. Continuing its local presence, it promoted parish credit unions in urban areas and supported the programs of the National Catholic Rural Life Conference, another midwestern-centered organization with headquarters in Des Moines, Iowa.

Father Daniel A. Lord, S.J., a native of Chicago, directed the Sodality of Our Lady from its national headquarters in St. Louis for a quarter of a century (1925-1950). He and his staff published the *Queen's Work* and other magazines and 240 religious tracts. During this time he energized units of the Sodality in almost all the grade and high schools of the country and in many of the parishes. He organized a travelling summer faculty of theologians, missionaries, social reformers and youth leaders that brought an intensive week of Catholic inspiration and instruction to all parts of the country. Half of the student leaders in Catholic schools throughout the nation attended these Summer Schools of Catholic Action. The diocesan directors of Sodalities formed a conference for mutual discussion and always chose as their leader a talented midwesterner, Father Joseph Hughes of Duluth.

An associate of Father Lord, Edward Dowling, was the first priest to take an interest in and offer guidance to Bill Wilson, the co-founder of Alcoholics Anonymous. Though not chemically dependent himself, Father Dowling studied the Twelve Steps of the AAs carefully and saw a similarity to the program of the Spiritual Exercises of St. Ignatius, the founder of Father Dowling's religious order. Biographers of Wilson have recognized the Jesuit's help.

The *Queen's Work* was not the only nor the largest Catholic pamphlet and magazine publisher in the area. That credit goes to the Miller brothers and their fellow Redemptorists at Liguori, Missouri, near St. Louis. They put out the largest-circulating nonorganizational Catholic magazine, the *Liguorian*, as well as pamphlets and paperback books. At first Redemptorists did all the writing. But when the Liguori Press bought out the *Queen's Work* pamphlets, it broadened its list of writers to include lay persons and members of other religious congregations. Benziger in Cincinnati and Herder's in St. Louis had long been publishing books by Catholics.

Father Joseph Husslein, Dean of St. Louis University's School of Social Work, combined with Bruce Publishing Company of Milwaukee to produce the Science and Culture Series of books in the 1930s and 1940s that developed the first wide readership that stretched beyond strictly devotional themes. Typical of these books was Theodore Maynard's history of the Church.

A program of great value to Catholic education grew up in the 1950s: the Sister Formation Movement. Before that, many sisters went from their novitiate to the classroom with minimum certification. They picked up credits during the summer at various Catholic universities. Some would not get their degrees until their silver jubilees in their congregations. A new turn came in 1940 when Sister Bertrande Meyers, D.C., published her findings on the academic preparation of nuns in her Sheed and Ward book *The Education of Sisters*.

That excellent work alerted many religious groups to the need for a more systematic educational program for young sisters. As a result many congregations began to send their junior sisters for several years of college or university before entering the classroom. The Daughters of Charity, under the impetus of Sister Bertrande and others, as mentioned in an earlier chapter, set up a program exclusively for sisters at Marillac College, in suburban St. Louis. The school gradually gathered students and faculty members of other congregations. One of the most noted of these professors was short-story writer Sister Mariella Gable, O.S.B., whose students in Minnesota had already gained a reputation for excellent storytelling.

Though much younger than St. Louis as a city and an archdiocese, Chicago grew so strong economically and politically that its religious importance had trouble keeping up proportionally. But early in this century, religious leadership caught up. In 1905 Father Francis Clement Kelly, a Michigan pastor, began the Catholic Church Extension Society for the promotion of the Church in remote areas of the country. A year later Father Kelly located the offices of the society in Chicago. Over the years this society built many thousands of small churches in rural dioceses, mostly in the South and West, where Catholic resources and manpower were limited. The Society supported the clergy in those areas, aided seminarians, and recruited and trained lay workers. It published a popular magazine, *Extension*, that kept readers abreast of the Society's work. When Pope Pius XI named Father Kelly Bishop of Oklahoma City in 1924, Father William David O'Brien of the Chicago Archdiocese carried on this splendid work. He later became an auxiliary bishop of Chicago.

Indicative of Chicago's growing importance in the American Church, its Archbishop George Mundelein became a Cardinal in 1924, twenty-two years before any other city of the mid-continent had a cardinal. Chicago hosted an International Eucharistic Congress in 1926. Father Bernard Sheil, assistant chancellor of the archdiocese, became auxiliary bishop in 1928 and concentrated his attention on the Catholic Youth Organization.

All Cardinal Mundelein's successors in Chicago, beginning with Samuel Cardinal Stritch in 1946, were raised to the College of Cardinals. Such outstanding lay people as the Pat Crowleys in the Christian Family Movement, Ed Marciniak in a variety of social reform movements and Dan Herr with the widely regarded journal of review and social analysis, the *Critic*, helped make Chicago the center of pre-Vatican II lay activities. A priest of the archdiocese, Msgr. George V. Higgins, continued the excellent leadership of Msgr. John A. Ryan as Director of the Social Action Department of the National Catholic Welfare Conference. His column in many Catholic diocesan weeklies alerted a wide readership to the current social issues.

Two Catholic universities developed in Chicago itself, De Paul and Loyola, and Notre Dame reflected the energy and enthusiasm of Chicago, even though some miles away in Northern Indiana.

St. John's College (later University) in Minnesota might have remained a regionally-influential institution among farm communities on those rich lands at the headwaters of the Mississippi. The return of Dom Virgil Michel in 1925 after studies in Europe changed that. With approval of his abbot, he began to bring to his fellow Americans advanced thinking on the liturgy. St. John's began the Liturgical Press, putting out a monthly magazine on the liturgy, *Orate Fratres*, later called by the term *Worship, Sponsa Regis*, a magazine of guidance for sisters, *Bible Today* and the *American Benedictine Review*. In another Collegeville contribution, historian Colman Barry, O.S.B., presented a balanced analysis of the attitudes and goals of German-American Catholics, thus paving the way for other excellent studies that followed.[5]

Spurred by these outstanding Benedictines, a St. Louis pastor, Msgr. Martin Hellriegel, introduced new liturgical practices in his parish of the Holy Cross in St. Louis and composed at least one hymn that survived the disappearance of the old hymnal. Gerald Ellard, Jesuit theology professor in Kansas, promoted the liturgical movement by books and articles and by classes every summer at the Summer School of Catholic Action. Many admirers of art glass expert Emil Frei, Jr., looked upon his work as part of the liturgical renewal. Following in his father's footsteps, he recaptured some of the medieval art glass techniques to adorn midwestern churches such as St. Francis Xavier's in St. Louis.

In Milwaukee, lastly, the Catholic League for Civil Rights, the first organization that set out to protect the public rights of Catholics, began its ever-widening campaign. Like the Citizens for Educational Freedom, it stemmed from the writings of Father Virgil Blum, S.J., of Marquette University. It remained under his presidency for many years. Recently it became, as it should have done long ago, a lay-directed organization. It employs a wide arsenal in defense of Catholic interests.

26

The Legacy of Pope John

Pope John XXIII lifted the hearts and minds of people like a warm west wind out of the Mediterranean. The first pope in 200 years who looked on the world with hope and optimism, the historian-pope insisted that the earth was a good place to live and men and women should make it an even better abode for themselves and others. He told the world that every day was a good day to be born; and every day was a good day to die. No Holy Father had spoken so optimistically about life for several centuries.[1]

When he was leaving Sophia, where he had been apostolic nuncio to Bulgaria a few years before, he had told his listeners: "Wherever I may go in the world, anyone from Bulgaria . . . who comes to my house . . . has only to knock and the door will be opened to him whether he be Catholic or Orthodox. He will find the most affectionate hospitality."[2] Shortly after he became Pope, people throughout the world came to realize that Pope John would be open to all whether Catholic or Orthodox, Protestant or Jew, Buddhist or Moslem, believer or unbeliever. He was truly the Holy Father of all people.

He brought back the confidence of the early Christians who looked on the message of Christ as destined to reach the entire world—a confidence that had been shattered by the advance of Islam in the 7th century. The sword of Mohammed threatened the Christian west for a thousand years and left a Christianity tied to one place—Europe. Even after breaking out of the semicircle of the Moslem powers and moving into other continents,

Christians, now disunited, could not untie the Church from their European place of origin.

Pope John opened new vistas, moved Christianity off its defensive posture, wiped out the beleaguered citadel mentality. He reassumed the stance of the early Church as defender of human liberty. He told his flock to look at what united it with its neighbors, not what divided them. Once his successor Pope Paul VI reconvened the council, after Pope John's death at the end of the first session, and called the late Pope a "Prophet of Our Times," many of the beloved Pope's views became the modern pattern of the Christian life.

The council brought a fresh outlook on the Church. No longer to be looked on as a vast, impersonal organization like General Motors or IBM, it was the flock whose shepherd was God, a field to be cultivated by the Heavenly Father, a sheepfold whose door was Christ.[3] Members of the hierarchy no longer presumed to identify the Church with themselves. Clergy and people were fellow pilgrims on the way to the Promised Land. The bishops, further, would share with each other the experience of their various regions. The administration of the Church would soar beyond the skills and outlook of a few higher Italian clerics and truly reflect the genius of all peoples.

Pope John's successors named cardinals from Africa, from Asia, from the Philippines and the islands of the Pacific; no longer would the Commission on Eastern Churches be composed exclusively of Italian prelates, many of whom had never in their lives traveled beyond their own limited areas, as it was at the inaugural of Pope John. The bishops would meet regularly in synods, and their wisdom and experience would enrich the Church beyond their dioceses. The recognition of national conferences of bishops as reasonable instrumentalities for the governance of the Church suggested that local men would handle local problems. No longer would a man who did not know whether Walla-Walla was an animal in Australia or a town in Oregon Territory make it a bishopric before the cities of St. Paul, Cleveland, or San Francisco, or create the archdiocese of Oregon City before New York, or Philadelphia, the nation's most populous cities, became archdioceses.

Twenty years before, Pope Pius XII had opened up the study of scripture to Catholic scholars, removing the barriers that his predecessor St. Pius X had set up early in the century. Now scripture would move to a more central position in the religious life of the Catholic people. Scholars of all faiths looked at what the sacred authors were aiming to do. They probed what type of message those ancient writers were giving, whether story, parable or poetry. They studied what the sociological background of the times might have been, and what the words meant in that context. New translations of the Bible were available, ones that all scholars accepted.

The Liturgy of the Mass saw many changes: the introduction of the vernacular in the forepart of the service; a choice of four canons; the enlarging of the scope of scripture readings to include three-year alternative selections, so that in this cycle the worshipers would have had contact with much of the New Testament. The Divine Office of the priest was simplified and shortened and recommended also to the laity as the prayer of the whole Church. The readings included passages from scripture and a wide passel of Church Fathers.

The Council called on the laity to take its part in the work of the Church. This recommendation had special import for America since the GI bill had given opportunities for a college education to countless men and women, and, for the first time in history, the Church could truly boast a well-educated laity. People in the parishes talked of wider participation in those affairs of the Church that immediately concerned them. Euphoria swept through much of the Catholic community.

27

Vatican II
Faces Human Liberty

What may best be called "the infallibility fallout" created a mind-set among American Catholics that made them utterly unready for Pope John's call for a Second Vatican Council. The fathers of the First Vatican Council had defined the pope's utterances as infallible in a limited way, namely when he spoke as pope to the entire Church on matters of faith and morals.

At Vatican I, a council father, responding to Archbishop Kenrick's rejection of infallibility, stated that every Catholic in Ireland believed in papal infallibility. The St. Louis Archbishop retorted that this was a tribute to the piety of the Irish faithful, rather than a recognition of any scriptural, historical or theological expertise. By the 1960s, the average Irish-American and most other members of the American Catholic body took it for granted that the pope was right on all questions. And many Protestant-Americans presumed this to be Catholic doctrine.

Little wonder then that every thought emanating from the least important Roman congregation had the authority of Sinai. And the average diocesan chancery official seemed to expect a similar acceptance by the faithful of all statements from his office. In some dioceses a group of Catholics could not organize as a social club without clearing with the chancery. Even worse, most chancery officials thought their procedures the way of all dioceses during all time.

Such church regulations as abstinence on Friday seemed as important to the life of a Catholic as fidelity to his/her spouse. For a layman to touch a sacred vessel at Mass was hardly less evil than laying violent hands on one's bishop. A married clergy was an abomination. Latin was an indispensable, sacred language that sealed the unity of the one, holy, catholic and apostolic church. The slightest modification of any practice, no matter what its historical origin or ancient meaning—even if these had lost their validity—would shake the edifice like a nine-point quake on the Richter Scale.

One of the leading American cardinals, speaking to members of a religious order between the First and Second Sessions of the Council, remarked frankly: "We went over to find out what Rome wanted. Only after we got there did we realize that we ought to say something."

True, a writer for the *New Yorker* magazine, who called himself Xavier Rynne, tried to alert American Catholics that something was afoot. And a young Swiss theologian suggested that the valid issues brought up by the Protestant reformers four centuries before ought to be faced head on. But only a limited number of alert Americans read these treatises. And a brilliant eastern bishop, looked upon even by midwestern cardinals as their theological leader, dismissed the Swiss theologian as one whose views were totally peripheral to the Council. He hoped that the young Switzer would be able to explain the mind of the Council to the "brooding Nordics," as he had attempted to explain the "brooding Nordics" to the "lucid Romans."

It should have come as no surprise, then, that the new "thrusts" of Vatican II, even though so many of them were long overdue, found the American Catholic body unprepared.

Between the first and second sessions of the Council, two dramatic events took place. On April 4, 1964 Francis Cardinal Spellman of New York gained the appointment of the most prominent American theologian on the issues of freedom, John Courtney Murray, as a council *peritus*, or expert. Rome had silenced Father Murray several years before, reprobating his early writings and forbidding him to publish in the future. In this instance, the wise Spellman won his appointment on the evasive tack that Jesuits deserved more chance to take part. On April 11th Pope John XXIII issued a most progressive encyclical letter *Pacem in Terris* (Peace on Earth). It called on the Church to countermarch to its ancient stance in the days of the Roman Empire as the defender of the freedom of people.

This encyclical approved many devices the Founding Fathers of America introduced to insure the liberties of our people. One of these stratagems called for a limitation of the time the executive could serve in office. After four years, he had to face the decision of the people whether to continue or hand over the office to a successor. Pope John approved this: "The fact that ministers of government hold office for a limited time keeps them from growing stale and allows for their replacements in accordance with the demands of social progress."[1]

All Americans, poor and rich, colonial daughters and sons of immigrants, Ph.D.'s as well as unskilled laborers, have varied opportunities to participate in government. They can vote; they can hold office; they can make their viewpoints known to their representatives; they can present testimony at hearings of legislatures. In some of the 50 states, citizens can initiate legislation or hold referenda to change laws or recall unsatisfactory officials.

Pope John XXIII praised popular participation in government in *Pacem in Terris*: "It is in keeping with their dignity as persons that human beings should take an active part in government. In this situation, those who administer the government come into frequent contact with the citizens, and it is thus easier for them to learn what is really needed for the common good."[2]

In the paragraph of the encyclical immediately following the above quotation, the Holy Father singled out for particular praise two other institutions that have been a part of the American nation since its outset: "a charter of fundamental human rights," and "a document, called the Constitution, that determines the respective spheres, the mutual relationships and the systems which the administrators should follow."[3]

In a passage that could have wider repercussions for human freedom than any other in the long history of encyclicals, *Pacem in Terris* stated: "Every human being has the right to honor God according to the dictates of an upright conscience, and therefore the right to worship God privately and publicly."[4]

This last statement reflected the mind of the early Christians who demanded freedom for themselves in the face of the all-powerful emperors of Rome. It was a simple, obvious statement to every American; yet a staggering thought to traditional European Catholics steeped in the absolutism of centuries. They could not answer it. They chose to ignore it.

As a result, when the American bishops wished to discuss freedom of worship at Vatican II, they faced Machiavellian tactics and, on a rare occasion, even deceit. Reactionaries in the Roman Curia had already silenced those theologians who had strongly supported a new resolution of the issue. When the discussion opened, the supporters of religious liberty were not cast as defenders of the teaching of the encyclical of Pope John XXIII but as opponents of an unassailable doctrine handed down from the past.

In an interview at the outset of the second session, Father Murray stated flatly: "This is the big issue of the council in the world's eyes. If the council sidesteps religious liberty, we are done for."[5] He asked at least a reaffirmation of the doctrine of Pope John's *Pacem in Terris*. "The declaration in favor of religious freedom . . ." he pointed out, "is an affirmation of the dignity of the human person . . ."[6]

To explain the Church's hesitancy in so obvious a matter as human freedom, Murray pointed out to his fellow American— and to the rest of the world—why the Church was highly suspicious of the word freedom. He traced this misunderstanding to the violence and injustice perpetrated by the French Revolution in the name of liberty. He pointed out, further, that most of the European political movements that flaunted freedom on their banners in the 19th century stemmed in some ways from the French Revolution.

"The context changed radically with the rise of totalitarianism in the 1920s," Murray went on. "When totalitarianism posed a threat to human freedom, the Church rallied to freedom's defense. This defense reached a peak in Pope John's great embrace of freedom. It will reach another peak, I hope, in the council's reaffirmation of the right of religious liberty."[7] Murray gave the American bishops, totally conversant with the practical side of the question, a solid theological basis for their demands.

Many European Catholic leaders confused "freedom of conscience" and "religious liberty." The former is a religious matter. It sets down a relationship between the individual and all religious authority. It presumed both a responsibility to form such a conscience after an intelligent appraisal of all pertinent facts, and a determination to follow this conscience once formed. Its extensive ramifications required most careful study, and an exactitude of expression to obviate possible misunderstandings.

"Religious liberty" is a relatively simple civil issue. It simply denied to the state the right to make decisions on religious matters, except in those issues *clearly* and *directly* affecting the common temporal welfare. Such an exception in the history of the United States was the refusal of Congress to admit Utah into the Union until the question of polygamy had been resolved, as Archbishop Karl Alter of Cincinnati pointed out at the Council.[8] In doing this, the Congress was making a civil decision, that looked directly to the common temporal welfare— even though the decision did affect the religious orientation of many potential citizens.

A declaration on religious freedom should not have been too difficult a matter. It could well have followed American experience that combined division of function with harmonious cooperation between civil and religious authorities. No step the Council could take would have promoted a more ecumenical spirit among religious-minded Americans.

Many Council Fathers were anxious for the clearer identification of the Church with human freedom. The placing of the Church behind the aspirations of all men and women for human liberty and the proper constitutionalization of its exercise would most surely prove a great stimulus to freedom throughout the world.

American Protestant leaders saw such a declaration a necessary step on the road to ecumenism. One of them, Dr. Robert

McAfee Brown, concentrated on three issues in a January 1964 article in *Presbyterian Life*. The past history of Catholicism showed notable instances of persecution of Protestants in various places. The practice of some Catholic countries in limiting freedom of religion gave reason for a residual Protestant fear that when the Church gained numerically and politically elsewhere, such repressive measures would follow. Finally, the Church had made a few authoritative statements on religious liberty. Why not, he asked, clarify the issue once and for all?[9]

The opponents of freedom constantly delayed action on the question. At the end of the third session Eugene Cardinal Tisserant, the chairman of a four-man committee, permanently tabled the matter in the name of the committee. He had called the other members personally without notifying Cardinal Albert Meyer of Chicago, the fourth member of the team. Outraged prelates gathered around Cardinal Meyer and determined to take the matter directly to Pope Paul VI, John XXIII's successor. Cardinals Joseph Ritter of St. Louis, Paul-Emile Leger of Canada, and one or two others joined the Chicago archbishop in this meeting with the Holy Father and won from him the promise that the fourth session would take up the important question of human liberty.[10]

Cardinal Cushing opened the discussion in the fourth session by saying how happy all Americans were that the declaration had finally surfaced. Since the Church had always championed freedom for its own activities it should proclaim that what it asks for itself, it also asks for every human being. He cited the late Pope John XXIII's words that a well-ordered society sought to guarantee its members life according to truth, justice, love and freedom. The concept of religious liberty included these characteristics.[11]

Speaking in the name of almost all of the bishops of the United States, Cardinal Meyer pointed out that the decree accorded with Pope John's encyclical *Pacem in Terris*. It would also allow the Church to give an example to governments as to how they should treat religious bodies within their borders, and would further ecumenical dialogue. Cardinal Ritter liked the document's pastoral character, prudence and adaptability.[12] Father Joseph Buckley, S.M., Superior General of the Marist

Fathers, hoped that religious freedom would be based solidly on the duty of following one's conscience.[13]

Other American prelates who offered supportive thoughts during the discussions of those September days in 1964 were Cardinals Spellman and Sheahan, Archbishops Alter and Hallinan, and Bishops Primeau, Wright and Maloney.[14]

The Americans found hemispherical solidarity when Paul-Emile Cardinal Leger of Canada spoke positively in the name of most of his fellow Canadian prelates[15] and Raul Cardinal Silva Henriquez of Chile spoke in the name of 58 bishops south of the border.[16]

Archbishop John C. Heenan of Westminster gave a brilliant presentation on human liberty in the light of experiences in the Free World and behind the Iron Curtain at a Vatican Press conference on September 26, 1964. While the discussion of religious liberty came under the guidance of the Secretariat of Christian Unity, Archbishop Heenan insisted that the issue transcended Christian unity. Even if no one talked of Christian unity, the Fathers would have to address the issue of human liberty. He saw it as "a welcome sign that the Catholic Church should stand so strongly for religious freedom."[17]

The Balkans had a voice, too. Bishop Smiljan Cekada of Yugoslavia was less interested in *why* they declared religious liberty than in *that* they declared it. He further urged the Fathers to appeal to the United Nations for a simultaneous declaration of religious liberty in all countries of the world.[18]

Another Slavic voice with equal eloquence but even greater authority that stemmed from his time in a Communist prison, Josef Cardinal Beran of Czechoslovakia opened many minds to the need of the declaration by relating the experiences of his country in his own day and five centuries earlier in the years of John Huss.[19] Many Italian and Spanish Fathers dissented, but they had no new arguments. Years of living under dictators had presumably taught them nothing. Pope Paul signed the Document on Religious Liberty on Dec. 7, 1965. The voices of freedom had won.[20]

28

The End of Exuberance

After a few years of exhuberance, however, the great forward movement lessened in force, like an avalanche that had expended its energy. No parish or diocese really designated a clear-cut area of operation for the laity. The clergy always retained veto power—even on issues of predominantly lay concern.

When the bishops returned to America, few took the lead in introducing conciliar changes, and determining what should be taken up immediately and what put off until later. Programs of "Renew" should have come then, rather than twenty years later, though they would prove good even at that time. Some bishops were simply appalled at the antics of a few, for instance, those who emphasized the banquet aspects of the Holy Mass at the expense of the aura of respect previously given to the Blessed Sacrament. Some wanted worship in the school cafeteria or in any hall but a church. At least one woman theologian said that the assembly could choose anyone as celebrant or "presider of the liturgy," herself or a priest, or any other person present.

Little wonder that many bishops worried over developments. But too few took a decisive lead. They reprimanded liberal priests but were inclined to ignore those pastors who denounced the council from their pulpits "as the greatest mistake in the history of the Church, called on a whim by a aging pontiff."

Some few Catholics thought the council a disaster; at least one bishop and many priests believed the new liturgy heretical and invalid; others felt that the Church had been on the road to its greatest period in history and Vatican II sent it on an unpaved side road leading to confusion; people who were most strong in asserting the authority of Rome over the Church denied implicitly the power of general council to do what the Pope and the Council had done.

Pope Paul permitted many priests and religious to return to lay life, and allowed priests who had earlier left the ministry and married, to reconcile themselves with the Church. One procedure in laicization of clergymen caused scandal. A priest who entered a civil marriage—ecclesiastically a sacrilegious union—was more readily dispensed from his church obligations than a man who honored his promises but asked for a dispensation before marrying. His permission came slowly. Some few priests dramatized their departure in juvenile fashion, to the disedification of their fellow Catholics.

Nuns discarded religious garb and moved into apartments. Some lived alone. They moved out of their traditional and routine apostolates into more direct contact with people. In living like members of secular institutes, some were actually returning to the spirit of their founder. Catherine McAuley, the organizer of the Sisters of Mercy, had not intended to form a religious order. In her plans, she anticipated by a century the way of the secular institutes approved by Pope Pius XII after World War II. Highly critical priests and her archbishop demanded that, if she desired to work for the sick poor, she become a nun. Prodded by their insistence, she made a year's novitiate in a Presentation Convent, but took her vows as a member of a congregation that by then she had decided to form.

Another devout woman, Mother Katrina Kaspar, started a congregation, the Poor Handmaids of Christ, to staff small inner-city centers of concern, comparable to the Hull House started in Chicago by Jane Adams. Within a century, church law had so redirected her congregation that the sisters ran schools and hospitals (institutes she wanted to avoid in forming her congregation) but not the social centers she formed the institute to staff.

"Collegiality" seemed to be a magic word, along with "meaningful" in the years immediately after the Council. Catholics on all levels in seminaries, convents and parishes met to discuss their problems. Yet one looked in vain to find a bishop or a religious superior of men who actually designated an area of decision for the people who discussed the issues. Many in authority seemed to think they were betraying ancient traditions if they allowed the lay artists of the parish to decide even the colors of the paint on the church walls, or the women's club to form a Brownie troop in the parish.

The bishops found out, too, that they were losing the voice they thought they had gained at Vatican II, vis-a-vis the Roman bureaucrats. At the council they had demanded first of all the opportunity to have a say in determining synodal procedures. At the international synods after the Council, Rome dictated the agenda and directed the trend of the discussion. Bishops found that collegiality came only with difficulty to their European counterparts who had grown up in totalitarian tyrannies.

Dioceses and orders spoke of consultation in the choice of bishops and religious superiors. Priests and members of religious orders responded enthusiastically with the names of men they thought qualified and lists of qualities they thought needed in their situation. Instead of a gradual strengthening and constitutionalizing of these procedures, even the most hopeful saw a slow eroding of even the consultative sphere. Individuals could take part constitutionally in the election of their mayor. They had nothing to say about the one who might be guiding their parish and diocese for the remainder of their lives. They might be getting an Ambrose or an Augustine or simply a man an unsure new archbishop in an eastern metropolis wanted to "ship out." An English Caribbean colony got a missionary bishop appointed for Iraq. France demanded a traditional "right" to name bishops for the Near East and rejected him.

The Machiavellian maneuvers of some of the curial cardinals before and during the Council had disedified many people. These lay people came to feel that Rome unnecessarily manipulated their lives. After the Council Pope Paul set up a commission of clergy and laity to study all aspects of contraception in the light of modern science and traditional morality. Many participants in the discussion felt that the Church had concentrated excessively on the physical act of union to the neglect of other aspects of the marriage bond. Many pastors asked: if such actions as lying and killing have various degrees of guilt, depending on object, end and circumstances, why did the morality of contraception derive entirely from the act itself and in no way from the reasons and the circumstances of the involved partners?

Pope Paul had called the conferees, according to several prominent American moral theologians, under the presumption that a certain method of birth control would prove morally acceptable. When these moral theologians convinced him that he had to reject that method, the Pope felt he could not countermarch from the teaching of his predecessors.

Many people, not distinguishing between laws of the Church and the laws of God, felt that if the language of the Mass or the laws of fasting were changed, then other laws could be changed. Many priests and seminarians had accepted celibacy years before only as a path to the priesthood. Theologians began to speak of two calls: one to the priesthood and another to celibacy. Many wondered if the western Church might not follow the practice of the eastern Church, and allow marriage for those who so wished. They recognized that celibacy did not automatically lead a priest to love for the many in place of the special concern for wife and children. Celibacy might lead to sanctity, but it could also lead to crotchety bachelorhood. Not all celibates gave themselves in loving service to God and neighbor. Rome seemed to think that in time such questions would go away.

The Council had looked to a number of legitimate demands of the Protestant reformers: greater emphasis on the Word of God, the centrality of Christ in devotion, the vernacular in Church worship. It no longer demanded that Catholic rulers restrict the public exercise of other forms of religious worship. It denounced anti-Semitism. It called on Catholics to assume a more sympathetic appreciation of the sincere beliefs and approaches of other religious groups.

As time went on, Catholics looked in vain for a reciprocative stance on the part of other religions. Protestants had applauded the Council's concern for freedom of religion. But few of them insisted that rulers of their denomination give freedom to Catholics in those countries where preference in law for a Protestant religion had endured. In a truly ecumenical spirit a prominent Catholic publishing house put out a book on the Catholic Church in America, as Protestant and Jewish individuals saw it. Catholics waited in vain for a Protestant publishing house to issue a book on the Protestant community as Jews and Catholics saw it. No Jewish publishing house reciprocated with a book on the American Jewry as Protestants and Catholics saw it.

Few protestants made any effort, except some groups in Germany, to explore those Bible texts that Catholics cherished, such as Christ's wish that his followers be one in unity and that he would build his Church on Peter the Rock.

Many individual Catholics gradually came to assume that it did not matter what one believed, as long as one was sincere in those beliefs. Many Protestants, in turn, simply looked on the entire conciliar effort as a four-centuries-late attempt of Catholics to catch up with them. Mainline Protestant denominations made little effort to lessen the anti-Catholicism that continued among their co-religionists who were fundamentalists. Preachers in the "Bible Belt" of the United States, for instance, still denounced the Pope as anti-Christ and had their match among the Orangemen in Northern Ireland. The media lords endlessly called attention to the millions of Jews wiped out in the pogroms of the European dictators, but rarely mentioned that even more millions of Christians, Catholics, Lutherans and Orthodox were slaughtered at the same time.

It was rare that an American Catholic ever challenged American Protestants or Jews to face historical realities, as Father Hans Küng did in a talk at Southern Illinois University in Edwardsville several years ago. "Our Lutheran brethren," he insisted, "cannot be satisfied to read Paul, Augustine and Friar Martin and neglect all the other Fathers of the Church. And our Jewish brethren must face up to the historical person of Jesus. Few dare to do so, but they must, if they wish to serve God with total sincerity."

Counterbalancing the great liturgical gains at the Council, were significant losses. The total rejection of the Latin liturgy cut the West off from a great musical tradition. Even that devout Lutheran Johann Sebastian Bach had written music for Mass. In emphasizing the banquet aspects of the Mass, further, many denigrated the sacrificial aspects of the ceremony.

The traditional silence in the presence of the Blessed Sacrament disappeared from many churches. Even though the post-conciliar documents on the liturgy reaffirmed the spiritual value of prayer before the Blessed Sacrament, few people stopped in church or chapel for a visit. An entire generation seemed to ignore the teaching of the Council Fathers on devotion to Mary, the Mother of the Redeemer.

The Fathers of the Council made strong efforts to establish their prerogatives in the face of a seemingly arrogant Roman curia. The reemphasis on collegiality, so little heard for a century, strengthened their position—at least for a few years. Unfortunately, the Church still clung to the administrative system set up by its greatest enemy, the Roman Emperor Diocletian, the highly centralized system recognized as military despotism when imposed on a nation. The experiences of the free world penetrated and inspirited Pope John XXIII's encyclical *Pacem in Terris*. But they never touched the outmoded administrative structure of the Church. College freshmen would shake their heads in dismay to find out that Philip II in Madrid would have to give orders to the Lieutenant Governor in Santa Fe, New Mexico. Could one criticize them for being amazed that some cardinal who did not know where New Mexico was should pick the new bishop of Las Cruces? The modernization and decentralization of the church administration should have been one of the priorities of the council. That it was not proved to be one of the factors that paved the way for the eventual blunting of the council's initial thrusts.

If these internal problems were not enough to challenge the leadership of the American Church, Rome hit the country hard with a semi-repudiation of one of the most popular and dedicated prelates of the West, Archbishop Raymond Hunthausen of

Seattle. He had not been morally derelict. Rather, he had, allegedly, been excessively lenient and forgiving with some wayward individuals. After long confusion, Roman officialdom eased out of the situation with a compromise. But the widespread confusion had caused great harm.

Even more trouble for Catholics came with the decline in public morals. Social observers attribute the letdown to many factors: the assassinations of President Kennedy, his brother Robert, and the Rev. Martin Luther King; the war in Southeast Asia; the misuse of authority by the central government in the Vietnam War, and by state governments in resisting justice for the blacks; and a resulting "doing one's thing" spirit among the young that succeeded the great youthful response of an earlier group of American youth to President Kennedy's challenge to "ask not what your country can do for you, but what you can do for your country."

While churchmen urged the authorities of the state to respect human rights and to insure that freedom the Church needed to function, they in turn did not introduce into their own governance all the ways to freedom they urged on their civil counterparts. The great constitution on human liberty seemed to end at the door of the church. Professor James Gaffney of Loyola University, New Orleans, discussed this contradiction in an article in *America* magazine in December 1986.[1] For the Church to live with this inconsistency seemed to show a basic dishonesty. Gaffney thought the explanation for this lack of integrity lay in the assumption that the Church's administrative setup was "as God-given as the Gospel and definitive as the creed."[2] Ironically, the Church preserved political structures, the result of "historical accident" and expediency, that were neither "invariably happy nor inherently immutable."[3] The Church could no longer afford to ignore in its practice what it recognized in theory as wisdom in governing.

"A doctrine of papal sovereignty" Gaffney pointed out, "no more automatically excludes representative government from a church than a doctrine of popular sovereignty automatically creates it in a state. A Pope could inaugurate a republic just as a plebiscite could install a dictator."[4] The French popular vote made Louis Napoleon Emperor in 1852, and an Austrian "plebiscite" welcomed Hitler in 1938.

Professor Gaffney concluded his article by quoting John Courtney Murray's preface to his translation of Vatican II's Declaration on Human Liberty. "The conciliar affirmation of the principle of freedom was narrowly limited—in the text. But the text itself was flung into a pool whose shores are wide as the universal church. The ripples will run far.

"Inevitably, a second argument will be set foot—now on the theological meaning of Christian freedom. The children of God, who received this freedom as a gift from their Father through Christ in the Holy Spirit, assert it within the Church as well as within the world, always for the sake of the world and the Church."[5]

29

Epilogue

The glories of the American Catholic Church are evident. Catholics kept the ancestral faith in spite of rejection and consistent pressures to conform to the Protestant pattern of their neighbors. They built an array of churches that made the inner cities of the north and east look like clusters of houses surrounding steeples with a cross on top.

American Catholic men lived steadfast lives and gave an image of Catholicism that appealed to people in a way that Catholicism in Latin America, for instance, did not appeal to men. They took part in every great American effort in war and peace. American Catholic women excelled in many fields of endeavor, as well as in homemaking.

In political expression, Catholics strongly adhered to the more progressive party with concern for the problems of the poor, and continued this tradition as they rose in wealth and position. A surprising number of outstanding Catholic political figures had their part in social improvement in America at both the state and national levels.

American Catholics built an amazing school system on all three levels, even though they lived in the only country in the "free world" that did not give state aid to students in denominational schools. Many Catholic schools in border and southern states integrated their schools on religious grounds before the Warren decision of 1954, and thus led the way for others.

The vast mass of organized workers in the north and east preserved the faith and took part in their unions while many workers in Catholic countries of Europe, such as south and west Germany, France, Belgium, and Austria, drifted into socialism. Many American labor leaders came from Catholic backgrounds.

While the rich in Latin America were "devout Catholics" and political and economic reactionaries, taking it for granted that God intended the rich to be rich and the poor to be poor, many wealthy Catholic families in the United States fostered forward-moving social programs.

The Church in America, on the other hand, did not succeed for almost 200 years in convincing Rome that the First Amendment of the American Constitution reflected the best Christian thought. Even today Americans have failed to make European Catholics, except Pope Pius XII and John XXIII, see the universal value of American institutions as means of freedom and common welfare.

Even after Vatican II, with an amazingly well-educated laity, American churchmen have not been able to build a system, as Protestant Americans had done long before, that challenged lay people to serve the Church and gave them a clear-cut area where they could exercise discretion and leadership. Often enough the very individuals who most protested the excessive intrusion of Rome in local affairs never left to their own lay people even those areas of activity that rightly belonged to them. In short, we have not built a distinctively American Catholic Church.

These failures do little to diminish the great achievements of the American Church. They help to keep American Catholics looking ahead. They can be a constant reminder that more remains to be done.

Catholics stand in the same relationship to their fellow Americans as the early Christians of the 2nd century stood in relationship to their fellow Romans. The early Christian community, a growing minority, often misunderstood and regularly persecuted, but sure of itself, continued to expand during the first three centuries. It alone had the full answers to the basic questions of life that humans ask.

Inevitably this nation will go secularistic in spirit or it will become universally Christian, as the Roman Empire did. If the country is to go universally Christian, the Catholic community must combine the virtues of the American past with the vision of Vatican II. It will join with its neighbors in standing four-square for public and private morality, especially justice for all. It will present an image of an active laity certain of its dignity and capacities, a priesthood dedicated to sacraments and service, and a body of elders sharing collegially with the successor of Peter the Fisherman a type of leadership that reflects the image of Pope John XXIII.

This pattern opens its arms in welcome to all people. It looks to the things that unite rather than those that divide. It concerns itself more with pointing to the message of Jesus Christ in all its fullness and beauty than in denouncing those who might fail to see some aspect of that message. Such a vision of universal Christianity is the nation's last hope.

But we cannot say that the American Catholic body is the Church's last hope. The Catholic Church will go on with or without a great contribution of ideas from its American members. It existed long before America became an independent nation and will live long after the cities along the Potomac are in shambles. But Catholics in America have so much to give because they have gotten so much. They have taken part in a political development that is, as Lincoln said, the last great hope on earth; no doubt they could contribute much more to the spiritual development of their own and other nations. Catholics must respond to the challenging words of a Lutheran divine, Pastor Richard John Neuhaus: "This is the Catholic moment in American life!"[1] Since uttering these words, incidentally, Pastor Neuhaus has found his own personal "Catholic moment," and entered the Church.

Endnotes

1. The Colonies Oppose "Popery"

1. Ray Allen Billington, *The Protestant Crusade, 1800-1860*: A Study of the Origins of American Nativism (New York, The Macmillan Co.), 1938, p. 1.

2. Ibid., p. 4.

3. Ibid., p. 6.

4. John Gilmary Shea, *History of the Catholic Church in the United States* (New York, 1886-1892), p. 365.

5. Billington, p. 9.

6. Idem.

7. Idem.

8. Ibid., p. 16.

9. "Journal of Philip Fithian," quoted in *American Historical Review*, V (Jan. 1900), 297.

10. Daniel Barber, *The History of My Own Times* (Washington: 1827), p. 17.

11. Billington, p. 18.

2. The French Alliance Reverses the Picture

1. Billington, pp. 22-23.

3. The Carrolls of Maryland

1. Thomas O'Brien Hanley, S.J., (ed.) *The John Carroll Papers*, (Notre Dame, Indiana: The University of Notre Dame Press), I, 146.

2. Theodore Bracco, O.F.M., *The Pastoral Theology Problems and Practice of John Carroll, First Bishop of the United States as Related in his Letters to Rome*. Unpublished Doctoral Dissertation, Saint Louis University, 1990.

4. The First Bishops

No notes.

5. The French Residents of the Mississippi Valley

1. William Barnaby Faherty, S.J., *Dream By the River: Two Centuries of Saint Louis Catholicism*, 1766-1980 (St. Louis: River City Publishers, 1973), pp. 20-21.

2. William Barnaby Faherty, S.J., *Deep Roots and Golden Wings*, One Hundred and Fifty Years with the Visitation Sisters in the Archdiocese of Saint Louis, 1833-1983 (Saint Louis: River City Publishers, Limited, 1982), p. 37.

6. Catholics in the "Era of Good Feeling"

1. *New Catholic Encyclopedia*, (New York: McGraw Hill Book Co., 1967) I, 90.

2. Joseph B. Code, *Dictionary of the American Hierarchy* (New York: Longmans, Green and Co., 1940), p. 343.

3. Jay P. Dolan, *The American Catholic Experience—A History from Colonial Times to the Present* (Garden City, N.Y.: Doubleday and Co., 1985), p. 306.

4. Peter Guilday, *History of the Councils of Baltimore, 1791- 1884*, (New York: The Macmillan Co., 1932), p. 106.

5. William Barnaby Faherty, S.J., "Italy's Greatest Gift to America," in *Italian Americana, I*, 2 (Spring 1975), pp. 281-292.

7. Heavy Catholic Immigration Brings Changes

1. *Immigration by Country*, 1820-1970 (Washington: Census Bureau, 1975), Part I, p. 106.

8. Trends in 19th Century American Education

1. William Barnaby Faherty, S.J., *Better the Dream: Saint Louis University and Community 1818-1968* (St. Louis: Saint Louis University, 1968), p. 98.

2. Lloyd P. Jorgenson, "Historical Origins of the Nonsectarian Public Schools, the Birth of a Tradition," in *Phi Delta Kappan*, June 1963, pp. 407 ff. The University of Missouri Press published his book in 1987.

3. Ibid., p. 408.

4. Ibid., p. 411.

5. Ibid., p. 412.

6. Ibid., p. 410.

7. Ibid., p. 414.

8. Ibid., p. 413.

9. Ibid., p. 414.

9. Catholic Beginnings in Higher Education

1. Joseph T. Durkin, *Georgetown, the Middle Years, (1840-1900)* (Washington: Georgetown University Press, 1963), p. 20.

2. *Mrs. Royall's Southern Tour*, 1830-31, (Washington: Royall, 1830-31), p. 155.

3. Idem.

4. Faherty, *Better the Dream*, p. 121.

10. Roman Misjudgments

1. R. Aubert, Pius IX, in the *New Catholic Encyclopedia*, XI, 406.

2. P.R. Kenrick, St. Louis, to Purcell, Mar. 7, 1854, in the Manuscripts Collections of the University of Notre Dame, (hereafter MCUND.)

3. Kenrick, St. Louis, to Purcell, Nov. 9, 1853, in MCUND.

4. *Shepherd of the Valley*, Nov. 22, 1851. A reprint of the entire message appears in Shea, Vol. 4, pp. 607-608.

11. Catholics and the Civil War

1. Letter of Provincial, 1861, in Mo. Jes. Prov. Archives.

2. Mary Ewens, O.P., *The Role of the Nun in Nineteenth Century America*, (New York: Arno Press, 1978), p. 231. Chapter Five gives a fine view of the work of the nuns during the Civil War. Betty Ann Perkins is to be congratulated for her excellent Master's Thesis, "The Work of the Catholic Sister-Nurse in the Civil War," Unpublished, University of Dayton, 1967.

3. Sister Angela Heath, quoted in *Documents of American Catholic History*, edited by John Tracy Ellis, (Milwaukee: Bruce Publishing Co., 1956), p. 377.

4. Ewens, pp. 232-233.

5. Helen Marshall, *Dorothea Dix, Forgotten Samaritan* (Chapel Hill: University of North Carolina Press, 1937), pp. 220 ff. Editor Bessie Jones in her introduction to Louisa May Alcott's *Hospital Sketches*, written during the Civil War, pointed out that the great juvenile writer recognized Dix's hostility to the nun-nurses at the time. (Cambridge: Belknap Press of Harvard, 1960), p. xxxi.

6. *Cincinnati Catholic Telegraph and Advocate*, June 29, 1861. (quoted in Ewens, p. 228.)

7. *The Photographic History of the Civil War*, edited by Francis Trevelyan Miller, (New York: The Review of Reviews Co., 1911), VII, 212-352.

8. Ellis, p. 376.

9. J.L. Spalding, *The Life of the Most Reverend M.J. Spalding, D.D., Archbishop of Baltimore*, (New York, 1878), pp. 298 ff.

12. The Impact of Converts

1. *Newspaper clipping*, unidentified, in Archives of the Visitation Academy, St. Louis, Missouri.

2. *Catholic Newsletter*, I, 5 (Dec. 20, 1845).

3. W.B. Faherty, S.J., *Jesuit Roots in Mid-America*, (Florissant, MO, St. Stanislaus Museum, 1980), p. 106.

13. Vatican I—A Missed Opportunity

1. Corcoran, Rome, to McCloskey, May 25, 1869, in the Archives of the Archdiocese of New York (hereafter AANY), A-35.

2. Idem.

3. Quoted by John Tracy Ellis, in the Foreword to James Hennesey, *The First Vatican Council: The American Experience*, (New York: Herder and Herder, 1963), p. 12. This is one of the first balanced and objective treatments of the American participation.

4. McQuaid, Rome, to Corrigan, Feb. 6, 1870, in AANY, C-3, quoted in Hennesey, 126.

5. Idem.

6. Martin, Rome, to Perche, March 12, 1870, in Perche Papers, at the Archives at the University of Notre Dame, quoted in Hennesey, p. 127.

7. Idem.

8. S.J. Miller "Peter Richard Kenrick, Bishop and Archbishop of St. Louis," in *Records* of the American Catholic Historical Society of Philadelphia, Vol. 84, Nos. 1-3 (March, June, Sept., 1973), p. 103.

9. Sergius Boulgakov, *The Vatican Design*, (South Canaan, PA: St. Tikhon Press, 1959), p. 11.

14. Catholic Parochial Schools Take Root Slowly

No notes.

15. Americanizers versus Conservatives

1. Faherty, *Dream by the River*, p. 118.

2. Philip Gleason, *The Conservative Reformers: German-American Catholics and the Social Order*, (Notre Dame: University of Notre Dame Press, 1968), p. 32.

3. Gerald P. Fogarty, S.J., *Denis J. O'Connell: Americanist Agent at the Vatican 1885-1903* (Ph.D. Dissertation, Yale University,) p. 62.

4. Ibid., p. 61.

5. Ibid., p. 62.

6. Simeone, Rome, to Gibbons, June 8, 1887, Archives of the Archdiocese of Baltimore, 88-S-5.

7. *Catholic Universe*, Jan. 12, 1888.

8. Colman Barry, O.S.B., *The Catholic Church and the German-Americans* (Milwaukee: Bruce Publishing Co., 1953), p. 137.

9. O'Connell, Rome, to Ireland, June 11, 1891, in the Archives of the Archdiocese of St. Paul.

10. Barry, p. 137.

11. *Associated Press*, June 13, 1891.

12. Gleason, *passim.*

16. Catholics and Justice to the Worker (1880-1891)

1. U.S. Congress, House, *Investigation of Labor Troubles in Missouri, Arkansas, Kansas, Texas and Illinois*, House of Representatives Report 4174, 49th Congress, 2d Sess., 1887, pp. 468-469.

2. Terence V. Powderly, *The Path I Trod*, edited by Harry J. Carman et al., (New York, 1940), 380. Powderly to Gibbons, June 30, 1887, in Baltimore Archdiocesan Archives, 82-W-9.

3. James Cardinal Gibbons, *Sermon* in Santa Maria in Trastevere, Rome, in *Documents in American History*, edited by John Tracy Ellis, (Milwaukee: The Bruce Publishing Co., 1956), pp. 477-478.

17. Individual Catholics in Social Reform (1890-1914)

1. Richard Siller, *The Queen of the Populists*, The Story of Mary Elizabeth Lease, (New York: Dell Books, 1970), *passim.*

2. *Encyclopedia Brittanica*, Vol. 4, p. 179. (15th edition).

3. Terence Powderly, *The Path I Trod*, edited by H.J. Carman, H. David and P.N. Guthrie, (New York: 1940), *passim.* Powderly's Papers are in the archives at the Mullen Library, the Catholic University of America.

4. Elsie Gluck, John Mitchell: Miner, (New York: The John Day Co., 1929), p. 116.

5. Quoted in Carl N. Degler, *Out of Our Past*, (New York: Harper and Row, 1970), p. 262.

6. Ibid., p. 268.

7. Ibid., p. 349.

8. Gluck, p. 131.

9. Ibid., p. 130 ff.

10. Degler, p. 348.

11. Testimony of Dr. Ranger Curran, Keene State University, Keene, New Hampshire.

12. Hennesey, pp. 214-215.

13. Robert E. Doherty, "Thomas J. Hagerty: The Church and Socialism," in *Labor History*, Vol. 3, No. 1, (Sept. 1962), pp. 39-56.

14. William L. Portier, "John R. Slattery's Vision for the Evangelization of American Blacks," in *U.S. Catholic Historian*, Vol. 5, No. 1, 1986, pp. 19-44.

15. John R. Slattery, "How My Priesthood Dropped from Me," in *Independent*, LXI (Sept, 6, 1906), 565-571.

16. Slattery, "The Workings of Modernism," in *American Journal of Theology*, XIII (1909), 555-574.

17. Faherty, "The Clergyman and Labor Progress: Cornelius O'Leary and the Knights of Labor," in *Labor History*, Vol. 2, No. 2, (Spring 1970), 175-189.

18. John Tracy Ellis, *The Life of James Cardinal Gibbons, Archbishop of Baltimore*, 1834-1921, (Milwaukee: Bruce Publishing Co., 1952, I, 547-594).

19. Philip Gleason, "Frederick P. Kenkel, Social Critic," in Robert Trislo (editor), *Catholics in America* (Washington: NCWC, 1976), p. 236.

20. Idem.

21. *Catholic Citizen*, Jan. 30, 1915.

18. Catholic Colleges

1. Privileged Sources.

2. Idem.

3. James Hennesey, S.J., *American Catholics*, A History of the Roman Catholic Community in the United States, (New York: Oxford University Press, 1981.)

4. Paul A. Fitzgerald, S.J., *The Governance of Jesuit Colleges in the United States, 1920-70*, (Notre Dame, Ind., University of Notre Dame Press, 1984), p. 197.

5. Ibid., p. 204.

6. Ibid., p. 212.

7. Ibid., p. 213.

8. Privileged Source.

9. Fitzgerald, p. 197.

19. The High and Low of Catholic Grade Schools

1. Thomas J. Shelley, "The Oregon School Case and the National Catholic Welfare Conference," in *The Catholic Historical Review*, LXXV, 3 (July 1989), p. 451. This is an excellent discussion of the case, with special reference to the help given by the NCWC.

2. Quoted in J.T. Ellis, Ed., *Documents of American Catholic History*, (Milwaukee: Bruce Publishing Co., 1956), p. 638.

3. Gerald T. Dunne, *Hugo Black and the Judicial Revolution*, (New York: Simon and Shuster, 1977), pp. 264-267.

4. Virgil Blum, S.J., *Freedom of Choice in Education*, (New York: Macmillan Co., 1958).

5. Hennesey, p. 323.

20. Catholic Social Reform After World War I

1. *Report* of the Joint Legislative Committee Investigating Seditious Activities, April 24, 1929, State Senate of New York, 1:1139.

21. Catholic Social Reformers: Rural, Racial, Pacifist

1. Vincent A. Yzermans, "The National Catholic Rural Life Conference," in *Catholics in America, 1776-1976*, edited by Robert Trisco, (Washington: NCCB, 1976), p. 146.

2. H. Aubry, S.V.D., Techny Ill., to Glennon, Nov. 17, 1939, in the Archives of the Archdiocese of St. Louis. D.P. Mulbrennan, S.V.D., Techny, to Faherty, July 13, 1983, in Faherty's personal files.

3. Copy in the author's files.

22. Capable Women and Steadfast Men

1. Dorothy A. Mohler, "Jane Hoey and Agnes Regan, Women in Washington," in *Catholics in America*, 209-213.

2. "Pope Pius XII Honors Notre Dame," quoted in *Notre Dame Scholastic*, Vol. 80, No. 1, (Nov. 19, 1943), pp. 16- 18.

3. Interview with Bob Broeg of the *St. Louis Post-Dispatch*, May 11, 1984.

23. Ethnic History

1. Gary R. Mormino, *Immigrants on the Hill*, Italian-Americans in St. Louis, 1882-1982, (Champaign: University of Illinois Press, 1986), p. 219.

2. Idem.

24. American Catholic and Political Liberty

1. Carlton J.H. Hayes, Marshall Whitehead Baldwin and Charles Woolsey Cole, *Western Civilization*, (New York: Macmillan Co., 1967), I, 234 n.

25. Midwestern Catholicism: Distinctive, Dynamic

1. William B. Faherty, S.J., "Midwestern Catholics: Distinctive, Dynamic," in *Ave Maria*, 95:5-9 (June 1962).

2. *Interview* with Cardinal Ritter, Aug. 10, 1963.

3. Joseph Ratzinger, *Theological Highlights of Vatican II*, New York: Paulist Press, 1966, p. 22.

4. Ibid., p. 91.

5. Colman, Barry, O.S.B., *The Catholic Church and German Americans*, (Milwaukee: Bruce Publishing Co., 1953).

26. The Legacy of Pope John

1. For the basic facts of Pope John's early career, confer Alden Hatch, *A Man Named John*, New York: Hawthorn Books, 1963.

2. *Wit and Wisdom of Good Pope John*, New York: P.J. Kenedy and Sons, 1964, p. 34.

3. *The Documents of Vatican II*, edited by Walter M. Abbott, S.J., New York: America Press, 1966, pp. 18-19.

27. Vatican II Faces Human Liberty

1. John XXIII, *Pacem in Terris*.

2. Ibid.

3. Ibid.

4. Ibid.

5. *Council Daybook* (hereafter *CD*), (Washington: NCWC, 1965,) Session II, p. 223.

6. Idem.

7. Idem.

8. Ibid., p. 276.

9. Robert McAfee Brown, in *Presbyterian Life*, Jan. 1964.

10. Vincent Yzermans, *American Participation in the Second Vatican Council*, (New York: Sheed and Ward, 1967), pp. 619-620.

11. *CD*, Session II, pp. 35-36.

12. Ibid., 36.

13. Ibid., pp. 45-46.

14. Yzermans, pp. 643-664.

15. *CD*, II, 36.

16. Ibid., 37.

17. Ibid., 65-66.

18. Ibid., 37.

19. Yzermans, 621.

20. In an otherwise interesting and instructive book, *Theological Highlights of Vatican II*, (New York: Paulist Press, 1966), p. 145, a professor of theology at Tubingen, Germany, saw prelates of three countries as having a part in the declaration: Bishop Munoz Vega, a Latin American, Cardinal Beran of Czechoslovakia, and Cardinal Urbani of Venice who broke the solid Italian phalanx of opposition. The author, Joseph Ratzinger, later Cardinal, mentions no Americans! This omission defies rational historical analysis.

28. The End of Exuberance

1. James Gaffney, "From Models of the Church to Models of the Model," in *America*, Dec. 13, 1986, pp. 378.

2. Ibid., p. 379.

3. Idem.

4. Idem.

5. Idem.

29. Epilogue

1. Pastor Richard John Neuhaus, *The Catholic Moment*, Supplement to Catholic League *Newsletter*, Vol. 15, No. 10, p. 1.

Index